THE BIG

O

FAILED
VENTURE

Praise for *The Biography of a Failed Venture*

'When one becomes an entrepreneur, one must start with an assumption that anything that can go wrong – will. Also, when we fail, there is a tendency to externalize the causes of failure. Prashant Desai neglected to remember the first adage but has pitilessly analysed the reasons for his venture not succeeding by refusing to externalize the causes. A must-read for would-be entrepreneurs. The book underlines the need for solid expertise in all facets of the business, a true understanding of the customer mindset and requirements, a proper appreciation of the competitor's strengths and weaknesses, but, most of all, the need to temper enthusiasm and passion with deep knowledge.'

– ARUNDHATI BHATTACHARYA, chairperson and CEO, Salesforce India; former chairman SBI; member, board of directors, Reliance Industries Limited, Wipro Limited, Piramal Group

'The great Austrian poet and author Rainer Maria Rilke wrote that "The purpose of life is to be defeated by greater and greater things" and that, in essence, is the journey of an entrepreneur. It's a never-ending marathon with no end, several defeats and where the journey itself is the joy and the destination. Prashant is still on this journey because he is an entrepreneur at heart and brings his touch to various businesses. I have had the pleasure of working with him and observing him for many years. Watch this space. The best is yet to come.'

– SAMEER SAIN, co-founder and CEO, Everstone Group

'For every page that makes it into a final script, a hundred pages are lying crumpled on the floor. But they aren't worthless, as they paved the way for something better. Failure is like that, never the end but always a new beginning.'

– FARHAN AKHTAR, actor, director, singer, producer, writer

'Success is often about learning to fail well. One has to have the ability to let go of the unwanted baggage that failure brings and to learn from the experience and move ahead. My compliments to Prashant Desai on bringing this out so well in this engaging narrative.'

– ABHINAV BINDRA, five-time Olympian and
Olympic gold medallist

'Everybody reads many stories of successful ventures by entrepreneurs, not many talk about their failures! But failed ventures teach us much more about life, adversity and how to overcome obstacles and succeed. Every failed venture has many lessons. We need to have the courage to accept failure in our lives and carry on. This is a rare book where Prashant Desai discuses his failed venture and the many lessons it taught him. A brutally honest book of immense courage.'

– T.V. MOHANDAS PAI, chairman, Aarin Capital and
Manipal Global Education; former CFO and board member
at Infosys; co-founder of Akshaya Patra; board member of the
National Stock Exchange of India

'Everyone makes mistakes. Be it in cricket, business or life. It takes courage to share them so that others can benefit from them. Prashant has been fearless with his book, just like me. All the best to him.'

– VIRENDER SEHWAG, former Indian cricketer

'To fail is not a crime but to give up on one's passion after a failure is fatal. Prashant Desai's *The Biography of a Failed Venture* is a courageous step stemming from his reflections in the wake of a failed start-up. This book is not just a testimony to Prashant bravely accepting his debacle but is also his way of selflessly enabling others to learn practical lessons on coping with failure, learning from it and using it as a springboard to bounce back.'

– RITESH SIDHWANI, co-founder and producer, Excel Entertainment

'I have always known Prashant as a real entrepreneur in corporate India and wished him well when he decided to take the start-up plunge. Things didn't work out, he made mistakes – we all make mistakes. We learn the most from our mistakes, yet very rarely do we share them. It is very bold of Prashant to document the mistakes he made and share them in this very readable book. I hope many of us embark on our own start-up journeys but make new mistakes instead of repeating the ones Prashant made. Wishing him the very best in his future adventures.'

– ASHISH RAMESHCHANDRA KACHOLIA, founder and CEO, Lucky Investment Managers Pvt. Ltd

'We all make mistakes, even though we all like to think we do not. Whilst we all learn from our mistakes, very few consistently remember them. And even fewer share theirs. Through this book, Prashant has attempted to celebrate mistakes. He has shown us how not to be afraid of making mistakes, how to try and avoid them, as well as consistently learn from them. A lot of insights for budding entrepreneurs in Prashant's book. A highly recommended read.'

– ATUL KAPUR, co-founder and CIO, Everstone Group

'This unusual story of failure is really the story of all our lives – what makes us fail. It is important because it explains what we don't need to do to fail, written by someone with first-hand experience.'

– MUDAR PATHERYA, analyst and writer

THE BIOGRAPHY
OF A
FAILED
VENTURE

DECODING SUCCESS
SECRETS FROM THE
BLACK BOX OF A
DEAD START-UP

PRASHANT DESAI

HARPER
BUSINESS

An Imprint of HarperCollins *Publishers*

First published in 2021 by Harper Business
An imprint of HarperCollins *Publishers*
A-75, Sector 57, Noida, Uttar Pradesh 201301, India
www.harpercollins.co.in

2 4 6 8 10 9 7 5 3 1

P-ISBN: 978-93-5422-929-9
E-ISBN: 978-93-5422-860-5

The views and opinions expressed in this book are the author's own.
The facts are as reported by him and the publishers
are not in any way liable for the same.

Prashant Desai asserts the moral right
to be identified as the author of this work.

Typeset in 11/15.2 ITC Galliard at
Manipal Technologies Limited, Manipal

Printed and bound at
Replika Press Pvt. Ltd.

This book is produced from independently certified FSC® paper to ensure
responsible forest management.

To everyone who has erred

Kisa Gautami was a young woman. When her one-year-old son fell ill and died, Kisa was struck with grief. Weeping, she went to the Buddha.

Buddha said, 'Kisa Gautami, go and find me four or five mustard seeds from any family in which there has never been a death and I will bring back your son.'

Kisa was filled with hope. But soon she discovered that each family she visited had experienced the death of one person or another.

She slowly realized that death comes to all.

Like death, mistakes too come to all of us.

Contents

THE DARE

THE DETERMINATION (18 MONTHS)

Author's Note

'It is good to learn from your mistakes. It is better to learn from other people's mistakes.'

—Warren Buffett

Success is celebrated; failure is overlooked. There is fame when one succeeds; failure is shamed. While stories of success attract, those of failures are expunged. Success underlines what should be done; failure underscores what should not be done.

My story is not of success but of failure.

I started a business and launched a truly Indian sports brand D:FY – shoes, apparel and accessories, much like Nike – that failed.

My business lost Rs 30 crore (USD 4m) in 30 months, virtually wiping out all that I had earned for nearly 30 years.

I failed not because I did not possess the necessary vision, determination and courage; I failed because the number of errors in my business exceeded the positives.

Initially one wallowed on the world 'conspiring' against my business, that circumstances had been unfair in not encouraging a truly Indian sports brand to succeed.

After the noise had subsided, what remained were facts. I began to think: What if one had done things differently? What if one had listened to what data was telling us? What if we had not done ... What if ... What if ...

It was not one monumental error that had sunk the ship; it was a sequence of under-addressed leaks – not planning to fail as much as failing to plan – that had been our undoing.

One could weep over the fuselage or decode the black box.

When one did select to decode, new possibilities emerged: What if these mistakes could be documented? What if my failure could benefit others? And what if – and here it got interesting – this analysis could initiate a dialogue on mistakes?

I started to look for people who had no inhibitions in sharing their mistakes.

My research on 'mistakes' furthered my conviction. There is not much written on either the importance of sharing your mistake or on being wrong. I chanced upon a book: *Being Wrong: Adventures in the Margin of Error* by Katheryn Schultz. It provided insights on why. Error study practitioners are a motley crew (Schultz, 2011).

This is why: we are social beings; mistakes are associated with shame, ignorance, indolence and worse, moral degeneracy. Mistakes are associated with deficiencies, rightness with righteousness. When we make mistakes, we deny, defend, ignore and blame them on someone else. As a culture we have not developed tools for accepting our mistake.

There is no '*I was wrong.*' It is always '*I was wrong, but ...*'

We are mistaken about what it means to make a mistake. Meta-mistaken. Our brain receives 400 billion bits of information every second. It filters the important ones and stores them for prospective access. The brain's principal function is to eliminate the unimportant. It then tags experiences and stores them into long-term memory. What it does not seek to remember it stores in inaccessible files. Mistakes, accepting mistakes and sharing mistakes are stored in the inaccessible folder. Our capacity to forget mistakes takes precedence over remembering them. Mistakes are an ultimate inside job.

This is where this book is different. I chose to make it accessible.

We step in shit all the time. Shit happens. Stepping in shit is inevitable. Either see it as good luck or figure out how to do it less often. Same with mistakes. It has the potential to do good. For better or for worse, making mistakes is a companion. I have decided to talk about *this* friend. During the lockdown, I came to realize that there is no experience of making a mistake. There is an experience of *realizing* that I made mistakes. Mistakes are always past tense and that is the beauty. It is never that I *am* wrong; it is always that I *was* wrong.

Mistakes help us see things differently. However, we have to see mistakes differently first.

Hence, this book.

I remember a quote in the conference room at the office of the prominent investor Rakesh Jhunjhunwala (with whom I worked) that read, 'Good judgement comes from experience. Experience comes from bad judgement.' I believe the truth is only offensive when we are lying.

This is my truth. Honest. Naked.

My Life: A Stock Price

I invest in equities. I am obsessed with the stock market. I spent twenty-five years decoding stock price movements. Sometimes they made sense, sometimes not. Yet, when you zoom out of a stock price chart, it always makes sense. I developed a way to connect life to stocks. On one such instance, Kishore Biyani (Kishore ji to all who worked with him, including me) told me that life is a lot beyond the stock market and needed to be viewed through a different lens.

Little did I realize then that my *life* resembled a stock price.

Everyone's, actually.

If you start plotting your life from childhood, you will see a life graph emerge like a stock price. When studied dispassionately, it tells a story.

Life as a stock price

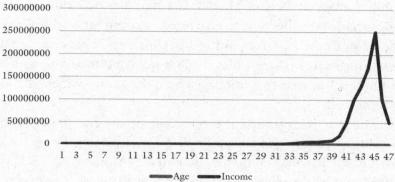

The X-axis is my age, the Y-axis is my wealth

A mere glance at the graph tells you a story. Age span 34–47 represents the 'eventful' phase of my life. The larger part of my life looks like a flat and dead line. However, if you zoom in (like in Google maps), you will observe that my life was a flat line till I was 20 before it commenced its upward journey. I lost my father when I was seven; there was no family wealth accretion until I began earning. The flat line too has a story to it, not wealth-wise but character-wise. You will read about this in the first part of the book.

The Desire (1–31 Years)

DESIRE: Childhood – Kolkata

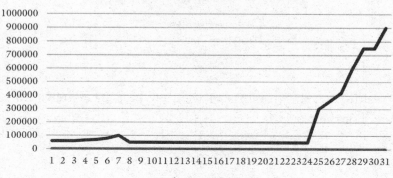

At 20, little did I realize that my life had entered a structural bull market. It began when I resolved on two things: (1) my decision to become a chartered accountant and (2) my decision to seek a career in the stock markets. I experienced a part of this in Kolkata where I spent my childhood and teens, and then I moved to Mumbai, where the action widened and accelerated.

Mumbai transformed the direction of my life graph (and wealth graph). It also transformed me as a person. From Rs 3 lakh in my bank account when I landed in Mumbai on 15 May 2003, my 'share price' increased 800x over the next ten years. *Eight hundred.* I was living 'the' dream. You will read about this in part two of the book.

The Dream (31–44 Years)

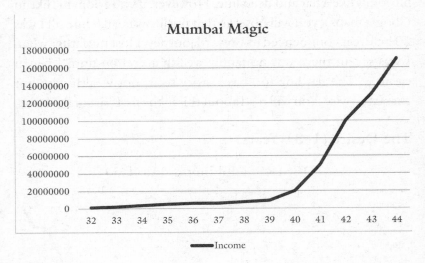

Wealth-wise, the years 31–44 were my best. They transformed me. For the worse.

I began using income, wealth and a professional career as the only metrics to measure my success. Most people feel happy, content, and thank life when it generates an 800x return in just 11 years. I felt hungrier. I wanted my life's share price to strengthen further. 'Why can I not go 10x from here?' I sought to fly higher. Faster. Farther. Took an outsized bet and lost it all. What had taken me 44 years to aggregate was dissipated in 36 months.

The first part of this journey was a lot of hard work and determination.

The Determination (18 Months)

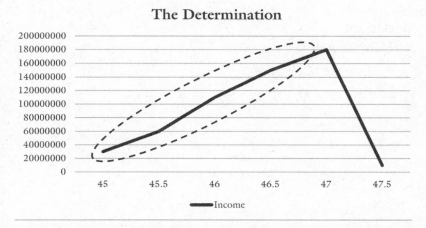

As I set myself for my biggest bull run, I encountered a wall. And after that ... *all the king's horses and all the king's men couldn't put Humpty together again*. I explain this in the last part of the book.

The Defeat

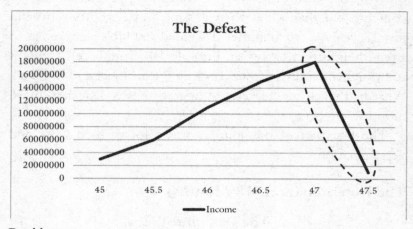

Buckle up.

Here we go!

Apologies (Not Acknowledgements)

A book on mistake(s) needs to begin with an apology ...

- To Kaavya, Arshia and Nishi (daughters and niece), my everything; the name of my company KAN DFY Sports Private Limited was drawn from the first letter of their names; I nursed a dream that when my company listed on the stock exchange, they would be invited to ring the opening bell.

- Mila (wife) for supporting a business idea that failed (the mood swings came as an undesired bonus).

- Ketan (brother) and Kishori (mother) who supported me and bore the brunt of a significant savings depletion.

- Bharat (late father) whose name I desired to bring back into the consciousness of those who had once known him.

- Aalok (late and lamented) and Mini, my closest friends, who welcomed me to Mumbai and helped me make it my home.
- Run-Fam, my 'family' of running friends who were the guinea pigs on whom my products were tested.
- Rajiv Mehta (my business partner) and his family, who lost a fair amount on the venture.
- Anil Kumble for my failure in not making a 'jumbo' success of the venture.
- Hardik and Krunal Pandya for the business not living up to their expectations.
- Utpal Sheth, Hiren Ved, Ashish Ranwala and Kavish Shah, who invested precious capital in solidarity and lost.
- Ritesh Sidhwani and Farhan Akhtar, who backed our passion.
- Team D:FY for abruptly shutting down the retail business.
- Justin and Jim from Brooks Sports Inc. as well as Laurent Antonio and Paul Giles from New Era (UK) for not doing justice to their brands in India.
- Every customer who bought from us.
- India for not being able to create a truly home-grown sports brand.

THE DESIRE
(1-31 YEARS)

1

Childhood

Honhaar birwaan ke hoth chikne paat

Dhanbad.

That part of Bihar where coal miners prospered. That part of India that inspired the Bollywood film *Gangs of Wasseypur*. That part of Bihar we generally referred to as the 'muscle' of Bihar.

I came into the world in this industrial dot on 7 January 1972 when incidentally, I was to learn later, Tony Lewis' MCC team was touring India and had just completed a Test match at Calcutta where it had been beaten by Ajit Wadekar's India.

How we got to Dhanbad is a story in itself. My father had been dispatched to Dhanbad to set up Bank of India's Jharia branch. What should have been a punishment posting was transformed by my father into an opportunity. The branch that he launched generated the highest fixed deposits across any

BOI branch in India. Some at the bank's headquarters probably asked at a senior meeting 'Why are we wasting Bharat Desai in the backwaters?'

The result was that the Desais – including their just-born – were soon taking the train back to Calcutta. The name 'Bharat Desai' began to figure with increased frequency in the Board meetings of the nationalized bank in Bombay (now Mumbai). In three years, the bank took an unusual decision: it would go international with its maiden branch in London. And who should they select to launch the bank? None other than the man with the golden touch who had proved his credentials in Jharia.

That then is the surprising story of my father: the man had refused a role in the family tea business to seek a job, inviting curious questions of '*Pottano dhandho muki ne naukri? Aa shu ...*' (Leaving one's own business for a salaried employment — what is this?) This time when he was on the verge of the biggest break of his career, my father surprised again; he turned down the offer to go to London.

The family was aghast; what it did not quite know was that my father nursed a heart condition, which was validated during the medical tests he was required to undergo before moving to London. Thereafter, it was professionally downhill; there was no cure for his heart condition in the 1970s; he lived weeks out of hospitals in Mumbai; he underwent two twelve-hour heart surgeries, and when he prepared for the third in May 1979, he turned to sporting analogy. 'I have come to Mumbai to play the third and final set of my tennis match. If I win this set, I will win the match and tournament.'

Dad never got to the match.

A couple of days prior to the surgery, I was smuggled into a Mumbai Fiat taxi that did all the familiar roads that gave me an inkling that it was headed for Bombay Hospital.

When I reached, the family was clutching to their handkerchiefs and hugging each other. Something big had transpired.

My father had passed away. Just thirty-six.

I was seven.

Poverty and Ambition

The Desais – we – were a fatherless three-member unit squeezed between three large 'families'.

My father's *kutumb* (family) comprised five brothers and three sisters. My grandmother was the matriarch – disciplined, loving, religious, well-read, industrious and strong on Jain values. In the absence of my grandfather, she was the family glue.

My mother's family comprised six brothers and four sisters. Her family had the largest tea business in India, and my maternal grandfather was regarded among the most respected tea tasters in India. The family was wealthy; it enjoyed respect, status and legacy wealth.

The third 'family' was the one we lived with in our multi-storey Neelkamal building in Kolkata comprising affluent businesspeople.

If there was one thing that set us apart from these three clusters, it was economic. After my father passed away, there was not much cash left to go around. The principal earning member had gone; what he had left – after meeting medical bills – was not substantial. We were like the family that is four wickets down in the second innings by lunch on the fourth day and needing to bat a day and a half to save the Test.

The result is whenever we engaged with the three families, things would always be civil at the engagement level. But there would come a moment in our engagement when the economic disparity would become apparent. Starkly.

We lived a hand-to-mouth existence on the interest income generated on the meagre savings left by my father; most others had prosperous businesses.

Each time the players on our team would order a dosa on the playground – a status symbol – I would turn to my tiffin that my mother had packed.

Each time the players turned to Thums Up ('*Thoda aur baraf dena* [Add some ice]') I would turn to *nimbu paani* (lemonade).

When friends offered a dosa or *moori* (puffed rice snack), one would politely refuse on the grounds that, '*Yaar, abhi batting karna baaki hai* (Buddy, I still have to bat),' whereas the real reason was that one knew that one would not be able to reciprocate.

At Diwali, neighbours burst a large quantum of firecrackers; my brother and I would make do with a palm-sized quantity and prefer to watch others burst instead.

At Diwali, when we went to the larger family's celebration, we would see relatives in their silks and finery; we would get two pairs of clothes that needed to last the year.

When we got older, our cousins graduated to restaurants, vacations and new clothes brought right through the year, and the 'difference' became increasingly apparent.

This difference was etched into my consciousness with precise words: 'They are rich. We are poor.'

The one daily occurrence in our lives was a recognition of how 'poor' we actually were. For one, we didn't have adequate money. More than that, we didn't have a father. I reconciled to not having a father for the rest of my life by the time I was in class VI and that he was not going to pop up one day in our lives; however, what I could not come to terms with was not having enough money. It was an insecurity that was to stay well into middle age. This low self-esteem would have an interesting fallout: whenever I was taken out for a meal by my one of my uncles, I would eat excessively – and be compelled to vomit by the time I reached home.

As we ended our teens, the struggle and strife of the childhood years would have a bearing on our personalities: my brother – who incidentally has played cricket at a high club level – was content with whatever he got. He interned at the family tea business, learning the fine art of tea-tasting and went on to have a chequered career in the tea sector. I was ambitious; I wanted to come out of the shadows; I was willing to assume risks.

I decided to take the road less travelled.

2

Becoming a Chartered Accountant

Saala mai toh saab ban gaya

1994.

My brother decided to marry.
We needed to renovate our home that was just the way it had been when my father had passed away fifteen years before.

My mother remembered: '*Kabaat ma kayi share mooeeka chhey. Bhaav kaadva padshe.*' (There are some share certificates in the cupboard. Check their prices.)

We extracted the share certificates. We made a list. We looked the newspapers for the prevailing prices. And totalled.

What we arrived at was a pleasant revelation. What we had in our hands was a value far more than we could have imagined.

Some shares were sold. The home was renovated. The brother was married. Many were invited to the reception. And even after all this there was a lot left to spare.

The disinvestment was not just a transaction; it proved to be an inflection point in my life.

The big message was not that my father had made a far-sighted decision that had bailed the family out at a critical moment; it was that the power of compounding – especially when applied through the stock market – could transform destinies.

In just fifteen years, the value of the family investment had multiplied 15x.

I decided what I wanted to do with my life. I had always wanted to make a lot of money without knowing how. I now realized that the vehicle of wealth accretion lay in front of me – the stock market – and all I needed to understand were the mechanics that went behind these sharp appreciations.

The result was that I read the *Economic Times* every single day to decode the world of business and finance. This was not going to be enough. Stock prices move up or down due to the demand for shares and their corresponding supply. To understand what drove this demand and supply, I needed to analyse businesses and understand their financial statements. That understanding would provide me with insights into companies that would make it possible to appraise whether they were worth buying into or not.

The result is that I elected a professional qualification in Chartered Accountancy and Cost & Works Accountancy in addition to my bachelor's degree in Commerce.

When my paternal uncle heard of my interest in stocks, he reached out to Sevantilal Shah, the senior partner of Stewart & Co., one of the largest stockbroking firms in Calcutta. Sevantibhai was a patron of talent: whenever anyone even as much hinted that *'Aapro Gujarati chhokro chhey. Intelligent chhey'* (He is an intelligent boy, a Gujarati like us), Sevantibhai would send his scouts to speak to the young man on whether a career on the markets interested him. If the young man even as much as nodded, he would be hauled into the presence of Sevantibhai who would impress upon him how the capital markets of the country needed bright young professionals like him.

So, when Sevantibhai was told that *'Bharatbhai no dikro'* (Bharat Desai's son) was doing his CA and CWA, there was no escape. Sevantibhai 'seduced' me into attending Stewart & Co. for no remuneration but for the larger 'compensation' of unlimited access to the prospectuses of companies going public, market grapevine and the Stewart infrastructure. In return, I was to use my analytical capability – derived from my CA and CWA training – to tell Sevantibhai that *'Aa issue ma rupiya lagaarjo'* (Invest in this new company going public).

Sevantibhai did one more thing. He called Mudar Patherya (cricket-turned-financial journalist) who was also one of his 'finds' and running a research desk out of Sevantibhai's erstwhile residence on Bow Bazar Street (a crowded neighbourhood in old Calcutta). I remember his words almost as if they were uttered yesterday: *'Muddar, hoon Prashant nay moklaavu chhu* (Mudar, I am sending Prashant). He is like my son. Use him in your research team.'

That explains how my structural understanding of accountancy was married to the real world of half-yearly corporate financial results. This is where I learned life's lesson that knowledge becomes power only when applied judiciously. At our research team, we would write down the financial results of listed companies on paper, use calculators to analyse, write commentaries on their performance for financial newspapers and engage directly with managing directors and chief financial officers of prominent managements.

As a part of Stewart & Co. one travelled to different cities and manufacturing locations to study companies bottom-up.

The more one engaged with corporate executives, the more one began to understand how commodity movements influenced product realizations that influenced corporate profits.

This extensive experience – day job, frequent multi-city travel – put a premium on my academic preparation. My usual day: rise at 5.00 a.m., leave for college at 5.30 a.m., finish college by 9.40 a.m., reach Stewart & Co. by 10.30 a.m., work till 5.00 p.m., then CWA and CA tuitions from 6.00 p.m. till 9.30 p.m., come home, dinner by 10.30 p.m. and then sleep.

For three years without a break, this was my routine. On the weekends, my friends would laugh seeing me yawn through the day.

The light at the end of the tunnel came when I was in the final year of my BCom course at St. Xavier's College in Kolkata. We were at a maths tuition in the Gariahat neighbourhood. Kishore Chotrani (a friend who eventually sat for the CWA exam with me) came in, excited, waving a newspaper. He shouted, 'Pudi (his nickname for me), we both are Cost Accountants!' I had become a Cost & Works Accountant at my first attempt. I was twenty-one.

'Let us go to college,' he suggested. 'The CWA Institute sends the rank holder list directly to the colleges. Let us check if our names are on it.'

'Rank-holder? Us? Are you mad, Kishore!?' I laughed and mocked. I mocked because I was never good academically, having failed in seven subjects in the eighth standard.

The list had not yet arrived by the time we reached. While we were enjoying samosas and chai near Delights (across the rear gate of St. Xavier's, often referred to as the 'back gate'), the watchmen beckoned. *Father Maliyekal bula rahe hain'* (Father Maliyekal is calling you), he said.

By the time we reached, Father Maliyekal was posting the rank list on the college notice board.

Kishore broke the silence: '*Pudi, tu saala all-India fourth aaya!*' (Pudi, you, rascal, have stood fourth in India.)

I went closer. I saw the name. 'Prashant Desai … All-India 4'. The difference between the first and mine was five marks.

I broke down.

Now came the bigger test of the CA degree – the World Cup compared to the Ranji Trophy of the CWA. In those days, barely 1 per cent of all students who sat for the CA exam passed at the first attempt. I was asked to decide – continue working, travelling and researching companies, or prepare for my CA degree.

I chose *both*.

In the confidence of youth, I stated that if I failed my CA exam, big deal, I never wanted to become an auditor anyway, but I intended to make a career in the stock markets. The result was that I worked during the day and attended CA tuitions in the evening. I missed my CA classes when I travelled (frequently) but returned, made up and took an office break a month before the examination.

I cleared the CA Final in my first attempt in May 1995.

My resume read 'Prashant Desai, Grad CWA, ACA.'

I was twenty-three.

3
Early Work Life
Paisa bolta hai

Now that I was armed with CWA and CA degrees, Mudar suggested that perhaps it was time I moved to a remunerative salary (at Stewart & Co., we were paid in 'experience').

He recommended me to Sumit Dabriwala of United Credit. Sumit ran a non-banking finance company (NBFC) and sought to start a research-based equity broking business. Equity research was relatively unknown in those days. Simply put, it meant researching businesses listed on the stock exchange, checking if they quoted well below their intrinsic worth and picking them for investment recommendation to institutional clients (or telling them to 'sell' if we found them priced considerably higher than we felt they were worth).

Considering that it was other people's hard-earned money in question, there was a responsibility in researching diligently. This

13

did not just involve examining the company's annual reports for clues about the integrity with which the management ran the operations; it also involved an examination of all that the management had committed in media interviews, engaging face-to-face with the company's senior management or interacting with the company's distribution partners. These interactions provided an analyst like me with a perspective of whether the company would do well or not and by what extent, the basis of all investing.

Let us take a hypothetical instance: research on a sugar company called Balrampur Chini Mills Limited (BCML). Research would commence with an understanding of the monsoons in Uttar Pradesh (more specifically eastern Uttar Pradesh where the farms that supplied cane to the company's manufacturing facilities were located). Research would need to estimate the impact of monsoon rain on the cane crop, the health of the cane crop in terms of disease incidence, the quality of roads that connected the farms to the factories, the way cane harvesting was scheduled across thousands of farmers so that there was never an excess of cane inventory waiting to be crushed, the company's capacity to work every single minute (all three shifts) through nearly six months of the sugar manufacturing season and the efficiency with which cane could be converted into sugar.

That would represent the operational side of the research. From a financial perspective, one would work at understanding whether the company had mobilized adequate working capital loans from the banks at a low enough cost to be able to stock a large quantum of sugar that had been manufactured (produced in six months but stocked for nearly a year).

The third part of the research would be the trickiest. It would lie in an understanding of the recommended cost price the Uttar Pradesh state government would put on the cane being delivered by farmers to the mills (in its endeavour to win votes the state government possessed a vested interested in raising cane prices year after year, a decision that virtually bankrupted the state's sugar industry).

Armed with this holistic knowledge, one would project how much the company was likely to earn that year and the next. Based on that projection, the objective was to understand whether the company's stock was quoted at a bargain on the markets or not and recommend a buy/hold/sell based on that to domestic financial institutions and foreign institutional investors (FIs and FIIs respectively). What made this research remunerative for a broker commissioning it was that the FI or FII usually placed a buy order through the broker, making it possible for the broker to earn sizable brokerage fees.

When I met Sumit who offered me a job, he laid his cards on the table; he confessed that his brokerage firm knew nothing about equity research and wanted me to set up a competent analytics team. In exchange, he would provide me a salary of Rs 3,00,000 a year, equivalent to Rs 32,00,000 today! (I stayed calm while he spoke, considering that until just a few years ago, our household would virtually survive on Rs 30,000 a year).

Sumit (and his brother Amit Dabriwala and his uncle Ravi Poddar) provided autonomy. I was provided an air travel budget to interact with listed companies across India (there were over 5,000 companies listed on Indian stock markets). I hired a competent research team. We engaged with several listed companies and provided credible investment recommendations. Based on our recommendations, we built an attractive institutional equities business.

The best part of working at United Credit was not remuneration; it was the opportunity to meet opinion-makers. One such opinion-maker was Utpal Sheth (currently partner of Rakesh Jhunjhunwala), who ran a respected research-driven company in Mumbai called HRS Insight. Utpal was not just well-read on companies; he could dissect business models; he knew several promoters by their first names; he wrote scholarly articles in the media. He had come down to the United Credit office to meet my cousin Kavish. My research team and I engaged with Utpal about undiscovered Kolkata nuggets (companies). Our conversation stretched into three hours over dinner, the beginning of a lasting relationship.

The engagement with United Credit lasted a few years by which time I decided I needed to earn better. The stock markets had tanked by then; United Credit could not afford to provide its research head (me) with a raise when it was otherwise downsizing; since I felt I could not really make do with an amount that was not commensurate with my increasing aspiration, I decided to look at other opportunities.

Coincidentally, Mudar entered my life yet again (after having introduced me to Mila who I married). He had started Trisys, a financial communications agency that produced research-based annual reports. This was a relatively new concept at a time when India needed to embrace global standards of information disclosure. Mudar was ahead of the curve; his company extensively researched companies and produced first-rate annual reports for select companies at a time when the common response was 'What good will such a report do for me?' In India, annual report was at that time seen as a statutory liability, something every company was compelled to prepare as per law. Mudar perceived this as an opportunity. He saw that the annual report was a transparent platform for companies to engage with their shareholders. He would engage with heads of every department within his client companies and ask them a range of questions, the answers to which helped him communicate the intrinsic realities of these companies to investors in a language they could understand (no jargon).

Mudar's communication extended beyond the printed numbers. He had developed a competence in being able to communicate a story that lay hidden between the numbers. He would extensively interview promoters, CEOs and other executives; he would present their organizational vision in a language the lay investor could understand. He would then marry this specialized content with world-class design. Gradually, the Annual Report began to evolve from being treated as a statutory liability into a value-enhancing tool. Mudar possessed the vision to have kickstarted the practice of a dedicated annual report agency providing a specialized service, a trend that has spawned dozens of companies dedicated to this practice in India today.

Mudar turned to me: India was at the cusp of strong economic growth; companies would need world-class annual reports to mobilize funds; the greater the capital appetite, the larger the need for analysts who could produce investor-friendly annual reports. He asked me to join. He offered the same salary I was getting at United Credit with an attractive bonus sweetener that would almost be equivalent to my salary if I executed well. I joined Trisys.

Mudar had the unique ability to bring the best out in people. One of the sharpest interviewers and writers I have come across, his company combined incisive content with world-class design. Since several Trisys clients were stationed in Mumbai, I would end up spending more than 100 days a year in India's financial capital.

My first-year salary and bonus at Trisys was 2x of what I earned in the previous year. I bought my first car (pre-used Maruti 800). In my second year at Trisys, I upgraded to a new black Opel Corsa. I fitted all the rooms of our Neelkamal residence with air-conditioners. I started frequenting better restaurants. I started wearing better.

One of the things that happened during my Mumbai visits was a realization of the difference between the equity research standards of Mumbai and Kolkata. The analyst community in Mumbai was professionalizing faster; the ones in Kolkata were largely ad hoc. The writing on the wall was that if one desired to build a career on the stock markets, one needed to be in Mumbai.

I left Trisys.

I had worked on one of the Pantaloon Retail's annual reports and engaged extensively with Kishore Biyani. I had casually indicated that I intended to relocate. I now spoke to him; he offered me a job to work directly with him in his Knowledge office in Mumbai.

I had just become a father; my daughter was three months old. I spoke to Mila, my wife, on moving to Mumbai.

This is what I told her: 'Kolkata is not the platform that can take me to the next level. I need to move to Mumbai, which is like an ocean. In Kolkata, I am like a fish imprisoned in the pond, intellectually and financially. I want to make more money for Arshia and Nishi (our daughter and niece) that will provide them with a life more prosperous and more comfortable than mine.'

Mila surprised me. 'I have lived and worked in Mumbai. Let us go to Mumbai, not because you want to make more money and provide us with a better lifestyle, but because it will provide intellectual growth. Besides,' she added, 'Mumbai will make you a better professional and we have time on our side to settle and find our footing till Arshia becomes older for school. Let us make the move now.'

What made the decision easier was that my closest friends Aalok and Mini (married to each other) lived there. Aalok (he left us on 27 February 2014) was ecstatic. I remember calling him. 'Prashant, *suppak* (awesome)! Can't wait. Great decision. Don't worry about anything. We will rent a house. Mila and Arshia will have all the support of our friends and families and we will go to Wankhede for every cricket game.'

I communicated the decision to my mother and called my brother in Glasgow (studying for his MBA). They concurred.

I moved to Mumbai in May 2003.

When I landed, the two people at the airport to receive me were Aalok and Mini.

It wasn't just relocation from one city to another; it was like the peeling off of skin.

THE DREAM
(31—44 YEARS)

4

Mumbai Magic

Yeh Bambai hai mere bhai, Bambai!

Mumbai.

More than just a city. A magnifier instead.

Where everything is scaled that much larger. Where dreams are suffixed with additional zeroes. Where you believe you have arrived at destiny's doorstep. Where the pursuit of steady growth is dismissed as a 'crime'. Where you believe you are entitled to become big, rich and famous.

When I arrived from Kolkata, the first reaction was fear. In my previous visits, I had warmed to Mumbai's professionalism. With that had come an unspoken apprehension. Mumbai is large, so one can lose sense of one's importance within the system; Mumbai is full of achievers of various kinds with no place for the average; Mumbai professes a high standard, so if one does not

23

raise one's game then one is history; Mumbai moves with speed, so one needs to keep running if only to stay at the same place.

I was relieved that I would not need to look for a job; I already had one.

I was relieved that I would not start like a nobody; I would work with India's most exciting retailer.

I was relieved I was not going to be lost in the crowd; I would work as the research back-end for the various ideas that crossed my employer's mind.

I was relieved I was not entering the Mumbai job market with usual competencies; I was an equity analyst-cum-chartered accountant who could also communicate.

The result is that whenever Kishore Biyani got a brainwave, he would call for me to work out the preliminary math and write out a note. My research and communication background helped me prepare financial models on the new idea with a note that connected the two. In those days (2003), Pantaloon Retail was valued at Rs 300 crore on the markets.

Kishore Biyani's dreams were much bigger than Pantaloon's profits. In one interaction, I said, 'Our problem is not ideas, Kishore ji, it is capital.' He replied, 'I know the problem Prashant, but what is the solution?' I suggested: 'You need to spend less time at the stores and more time at fund manager's offices.' He got it.

That conversation transformed my profile at Pantaloon. Kishore Biyani decided to pitch more aggressively to investors; he turned to me for investor presentations. He was a different thinker. He had read an article in *Harvard Business Review* about storytelling as a corporate strategy used in the USA. He had made two films (*Na Tum Jaano Na Hum* and *Chura Liya Hai Tumne*). He desired to become the first Indian listed company to leverage the storytelling-based presentation approach. He encouraged me to utilize the communications and design experience that I had learned at Trisys and take the Pantaloon experience ahead (Fryer, 2003).

Besides, given my equity investing background and my network across equity analysts, Kishore Biyani asked me to accompany him when he presented the Pantaloon story to investors – across India and globally. Since organized retail was a nascent sector in 2003, there was a premium on the need to communicate the company's multi-decade opportunity. Investors then didn't quite understand the concept of modern retail as a value-creation platform. That provided me with the opportunity to draw their attention to Walmart's growth and draw Indian retail and Pantaloon into the discussion. The result is that investors liked our multi-year growth aspiration. Investors and analysts (domestic and international) became familiar with me as I would accompany them on visits to our Big Bazaar stores.

The result: Pantaloon began to mobilize growth capital from investors.

Soon, Kishore Biyani realized that the time he could allocate for prospective investors was finite; he needed someone who could comprehend his vision, articulate his blueprint and speak with similar passion.

I was selected to be his alter ego when it came to investor engagement. I would speak with investors and communicate the broad Pantaloon story. He would come in and address the Q&A segment.

At one large investor meet, I plugged in for the second role as well. I answered questions confidently on his behalf. The investors didn't blanche; they didn't say 'Can we get a word in with Mr Biyani as well?' They took my word as the word of Kishore Biyani.

The upside of that engagement was not just the opportunity to speak on behalf of the company to a range of global investors; it was the opportunity to get into the mind of the man himself.

Kishore Biyani would share with me the importance of being a well-rounded generalist (not specialist). He encouraged me to extend my horizon beyond the stock market. He pushed me to open myself to experiences like art, music, movies and literature. He told me to research *Times of India* – how the paper covered topics of interest for almost every kind of reader. Just like *TOI*, he would say, you need to be a generalist. 'You are *Economic Times*, Prashant, but you need to become a *TOI*,' he would say.

In the meanwhile, the Pantaloon stock kept rising due to a general improvement in the stock markets. At peak in 2007, Pantaloon was valued at a staggering Rs 22,000 crore, up 70x from when I had joined in 2003.

As investor interest grew, so did my confidence, respect and visibility as 'Head – Investor Relations'. I began to be known as '*Woh* Pantaloon*wala*' (That one from Pantaloon). As a spin-off benefit, my salary increased 3x.

There was another spin-off benefit as 'Head – Investor Relations, Pantaloon'. While travelling to the US, Europe, Southeast Asia and Japan to present the Pantaloon story to investors, I would inevitably end up sharing a meal with a successful investor or analyst. I would start understanding their perspective on the global economy, on the India growth story, on the stocks they were prospecting and on emerging opportunities. I had learnt early in life (through my father's investment in stocks) that wealth creation for people who held day jobs could be largely achieved only through prudent equity investments.

Those conversations began to influence my investment style. I began to invest all my savings into equities. My bets became larger. A larger number of my conversations with analysts began to end with 'What should I buy?'

What strengthened my investing hypothesis was the constant commentary on how growth was stagnating in the West and how BRICS (Brazil, Russia, India, China and South Africa) was the place to be in. During those years, BRICS attracted sizable global money. Their stock markets strengthened. The value of my investments appreciated.

I didn't just seek to maximize returns from my portfolio of financial investments; I soon had a completely new perspective on life where I would seek to maximize returns from my portfolio of competencies. The bottom line: I wanted to make more money.

The opportunity for doing so did not come as much from a tip as much as it came from my network of friends and acquaintances. Utpal Sheth, who I had first met a decade ago and been engaging frequently with in between, now worked with Enam Securities, one of the most respected investment firms in the country. Enam was also an in-house broker to Pantaloon. They were our adviser on capital markets. Utpal led that team. Utpal and I were friends; he respected what I had achieved. One day, Utpal told me that he was leaving Enam to help the legendary investor Rakesh Jhunjhunwala (every one of his friends and acquaintances would call him Bhaiya [big brother], and so did I) institutionalize his business. Until then, Bhaiya operated out of a small office in the Fort area of Mumbai with two employees. Rakesh Bhaiya and Utpal were close. He wanted Utpal to set up RARE Enterprises, his firm. RARE Enterprises would never manage external money but would manage Rakesh Bhaiya's personal wealth with professional expertise. Utpal asked me: 'Will you join as Head of Research?'

Just seven words.

But in those few seconds I could see the opening of a large door that I felt could transform my life.

I am surprised I didn't jump at Utpal before he had completed the sentence.

I told Kishore Biyani all this (almost). He said something I remember: that over a longer period I would make probably more money at Pantaloon, but presently he would not have been able to match what Rakesh Jhunjhunwala was offering. Besides, he wasn't too pleased about my switch. He said he had invested extensively to make me the company's investor interface (I agreed); he had developed a trust and now just when I was at the cusp of delivering superior value to Pantaloon, I was leaving.

I joined Rakesh Jhunjhunwala (Big Bull) because he represented (and still does) the Great Indian Dream. His story of wealth creation is fascinating.

Big Bull was born into a conservative Marwari family; his father was a senior Income Tax officer. Rakesh Bhaiya was a chartered accountant who was more interested in investing and trading on the stock markets. He initiated his investing career with Rs 5,000, borrowed Rs 2,00,000 to commence trading (buying and selling stocks within periods as short as a day, week or month) and grew that modest amount to an estimated USD 4.2 billion as per *Forbes* in April 2021.

If Kishore Biyani was known to come up with unique customer observations and transform them into revenues, Big Bull possessed the ability to see the big picture of where the world or India was going. He would invest his trading profits into shares of companies that he held for the long term. For instance, he first invested in the shares of Titan Industries in 2003; he continues to hold shares in that company even though his holding has appreciated more than 250 times.

Big Bull bet big during Madhu Dandvate's game-changing Union Budget of 1989. He predicted a structural bull market following Manmohan Singh's landmark Budget speech in 1991 when India opened up to liberalization. He went on to correctly predict short-term price movements (trading) and long-term direction (investing), among few who could trade positions with speed and invest with patience, generally considered to warrant completely different competencies.

Big Bull was spot on. He continued to back the India growth story, transforming the risk-averse into equity investors. His initial corpus of a few thousands has grown to over Rs 30,000 crore today (*Forbes*) – conclusive proof that intelligence, luck and pluck can transform destinies; proof that modern India will throw up a new generation of wealthy super-achievers.

I joined RARE because I felt that some of his genius would rub off on me; that my ability to prospect multi-baggers would get a hydraulic impact; I could invest at the same time Bhaiya would and simply ride the wave; I could cash in on hefty annual bonuses to buy a house in Mumbai, and create a platform to scale my wealth to the next level.

Within two years of arriving in Mumbai, I was the Head of Research at RARE, Rakesh Jhunjhunwala's partnership firm. My job profile was similar to what I had done at United Credit, but this time the scale was different. My team and I had two objectives (or so I thought). One was to provide research and information on the companies Big Bull was invested in. Two, to identify new ideas for investment for him.

Unlike United Credit, the responsibility and the quality of research expected was more exacting. I was confident because my skills had matured. Besides, working closely with Kishore Biyani had given me an insight into how companies operated. I was connected with global investors as well.

Working closely with Rakesh Jhunjhunwala was a remarkable insight into the mind of the man who could sniff opportunity a mile away. There was a flip side as well. Rakesh Jhunjhunwala would often fly off the handle. After the genteel environment of Pantaloon, I found it difficult to adjust. If I continued at RARE, it was in the hope that at the end of the year everything would even out when I received a fat bonus that would make me wealthy enough to buy a home in Mumbai.

When the Big Bull heard about this, he lost no time in presenting an honest perspective: 'Prashant, there is no free lunch in life. If you want to buy a house in Mumbai, you will have to take your own risks. I won't give that much of a bonus for you to buy a house. You will need to use your intellect, take risks and create your wealth for you to buy it.' He explained it as matter-of-factly as he could: 'No risk, no reward. Risks and rewards are directly proportionate, unless you are lucky where you take a relatively small risk and create a fortune. As far as I am concerned, I don't like to ride the element of luck. I like to stack measured risks against prospective rewards and then take a call on whether to invest or not.'

Wealth, wealth, wealth. At RARE, we were talking about this all the time. Big Bull had a group of friends who would visit him. Besides, he would celebrate many events. We got invited to most. Most conversations revolved around the quantum of stocks each one had invested in. The numbers we would hear would be in hundreds of crores. Despite doing reasonably well in Mumbai, I realized I was 'poor' in comparison. There were people I met there who made vulgar sums of money. A stock that doubled in three years was considered to have under-performed.

This sustained exposure transformed my mindset. Suddenly the dream to own a couple of crores made me look like a beggar. The desire to become fabulously rich became a *need*. More than a need, it became an obsession. And soon that obsession began to acquire a number. That number was Rs 50 crore.

I began to dream about this number. I began to calculate the various investment possibilities that would get me there. I began to take higher risks.

Sadly, the meagre RARE bonus proved to be a dampener. I left RARE in less than two years.

I went back to Kishore Biyani. By then, Pantaloon had evolved to become Future Group (FG) and was expanding into media, e-commerce, financial services, branding and insurance. I told him I missed leading from the front. I missed the autonomy. I missed the excitement.

Kishore Biyani was welcoming. Between 2003 and 2007, Future Group had expanded rapidly; its valuation had climbed from Rs 300 crore in 2003 to Rs 22,000 crore in 2007. These were heady times. Kishore Biyani wasn't just growing valuations; he was virtually creating India's new organized retail sector by inspiring a generation of entrepreneurs who wanted to be the next 'KB'; he was rewriting rules; he was questioning paradigms; he was complementing labour with risk-taking; he was turning the old dictum of 'seeing is believing' into 'believe and you will see.'

I rejoined Pantaloon with a charge of my old function. Besides, I was heading Future Ventures and was seconded to be the interface between Future Group teams and Sameer Sain and Atul Kapoor, former Goldman MDs from London, to set up a consumer-led asset management business now called Everstone Group (called Future Capital Holdings Limited at that time).

Sameer and Atul were successful professionals. Both were different personalities. Like chalk and cheese. Yin and yang. Sameer was the risk-taker and painter. Atul was the perfectionist with strong analytical and process orientation. I had the opportunity to learn private equity investing from both, which I believe was a godsent opportunity in my wealth aggregation journey.

Two things happened at that time that need to be detailed.

One, I was aggressively investing my personal capital and extensively trading, diluting my workplace focus. Rather than confront, Atul and Sameer seeded an idea: why not start an investor relations firm that would advise listed companies in terms of positioning and investor interaction?* When I went over to thank Sameer for this idea, he told me something that I now value deeper. He said, 'PD, creating wealth is like running a marathon. The problem is you run it like a sprint. It can make you take high risks and shortcuts where you could often get blindsided.'

Two, I chanced upon Rakesh Jhunjhunwala speaking at an investor conference where he spoke about India entering a structural bull market. I recalled his 'risk-taking' exhortation; I did not just put my investable surplus into equities, but leveraged and betted far more than ever; I *played* the markets.

This proved to be a particularly challenging time for my wife and daughter (4+ years old). I was borrowing to place bets on short-term price movements. I would be tracking US markets at night in the hope of generating leads on how the Indian markets

---

* In August 2008, I started India's first IR firm dedicated to creating wealth for business houses by helping them understand the capital market realities (I recall Rakesh Jhunjhunwala's wisdom: 'Majority drives control, minority drives valuation'). My IR consultancy did well with clients like FT, MCX, Phoenix Mills, Prozone and more, but Indian promoters did not pay well for the value that was delivered and I eventually sold the business and moved on.

would behave the following day, putting me in a position to make a proactive trade. I would be bingeing on packaged foods through the night.

Looking back, I could have been wiped out if I had made a single large move wrong.

The reality was that I got a few moves completely right, exited the market and landed a substantial profit.

I bought a home in Juhu, Mumbai.

Finally.

5

Wealth Creation at FT

Risk hai toh ishq hai

When I commenced my Investor Relations practice, one of my first clients was Jignesh Shah (JS).

JS had risen from the position of an employee in BSE's technology division and gone on to create one of India's biggest exchanges and exchange ecosystem – Financial Technologies (India) Limited (FT), now listed as 63 Moons Technologies Limited.

FT was a unique company. FT had started as a technology company with a product ODIN, an exchange trading platform that allowed brokers to trade across multiple exchanges and multiple assets classes from a single screen. The business model of FT transformed when the Forward Markets Commission, the regulator for commodities trading (Government of India), invited bidders to set up a commodities exchange platform after giving three years to National Stock Exchange (NSE) to set it up (and failed).

The technology for setting up such an exchange was not easily available. Whereas other licensors scouted for outsourcing the technology, FT developed it in-house and launched Multi Commodity Exchange (MCX) within six months of getting the license. FT was the technology provider and promoter of MCX. MCX under JS's leadership created customized Indian contracts for gold, focusing on *tola* instead of ounce and 99.95 per cent purity over 99 per cent. MCX met with immediate success as hedgers and speculators embraced it thoroughly. MCX went on to become the world's No. 2 commodities exchange, beating three Chinese exchanges in under seven years, putting India on the global map. MCX got listed and the IPO was rated by FinanceAsia Awards as the 'Best Mid-Cap Equity Deal' in the entire Asia-Pacific in 2012. MCX also beat the NSE-promoted NCDEX hands down. MCX went on to set up an electricity spot exchange, Indian Energy Exchange (IEX), and again beat NSE with 97 per cent market share. It set up National Spot Exchange Limited (NSEL) and beat NSE with 99 per cent market share. FT got the nod from the Singapore regulator Monetary Authority of Singapore to set up the second exchange in Singapore called Singapore Mercantile Exchange (SMX). FT partnered with the Dubai government to set up the Dubai Gold & Commodity Exchange (DGCX). FT also set up exchanges in Mauritius and Botswana in Africa (MCX, 2012).

Even as FT was widely recognized as a pioneer, the company had a small issue on its hands. The company had failed to communicate its story lucidly to investors. The result was that a company that operated a transaction-led exchange technology product intellectual property company and owned nine global exchanges (including monopolistic exchanges like MCX, IEX and NSEL) traded for less than Rs 3,000 crore.

When JS engaged me as an IR consultant, his brief was: simplify the complex, explain the big picture and emphasize the technology uniqueness.

I would normally have recommended what I had practised at Pantaloon: conduct a roadshow for JS and get him to articulate his vision to prospective investors. However, the hands-on JS was too busy operationalizing exchanges and engaging with regulators the world over to attend to investors. He needed someone from within his company who was familiar with the investor ecosystem and could competently position the FT story.

He asked me to join as 'President, Investor Relations and Mergers & Acquisitions'.

There were a number of upsides in joining FT.

The stock was massively undervalued; there was a challenge to address.

There was a fundamentally good story to communicate.

The story was growing, validating the need for constant informed communication.

The story needed to be marketed to a national and international audience.

I sold my IR practice and joined FT in December 2012. I would be given a free hand to overhaul its investor communication. I was promised stock options if I delivered. This was a unique combination – a stable and fixed remuneration on the one hand and being an active participant in capitalizing on the upside in the event that I delivered.

In a lot of ways, I told myself that this was a dream engagement. I was riding a relatively unfancied Derby winner with impeccable credentials; I may not have been the jockey but was part of an ecosystem that empowered the thoroughbred to gallop faster. If the horse won, given the huge odds, the takings would be extensive.

Then came the tsunami.

On 31 July 2013, within six months of joining FT, National Sport Exchange Limited (NSEL), one of the exchanges owned by FT, was abruptly asked to discontinue operations by the Forward Markets Commission. This abrupt shutdown triggered a payments default crisis of Rs 5,600 crore (Sinha, 2013).

FT, the parent company, was singled out. A media trial painted JS as the culprit despite no money trail leading to him. There was not a day when the papers did not carry a picture of JS. The stock nosedived. The CBI, Enforcement Directorate and Economic Offences Wing pounced on FT. JS would be summoned several times for questioning (and even arrested thrice).

At that moment, a number of friends and family members suggested that it would be better to leave: *'Aa badhu kya sudhi chaalsey, kaai khabar nathi, chhodi de FT'* (No one knows how long this will drag, leave FT).

I knew JS well enough to trust my instinct that there was more to what media was reporting than met the eye. I also felt that it would be unprofessional to desert FT in challenging times.

I spoke to Mila, my wife. This is what I told her: 'Things are bad at FT. We are being attacked on multiple fronts – from the government, regulators, brokers, traders, the media and agencies like the Enforcement Directorate, CBI, Economic Offences Wing of Mumbai Police and Serious Frauds Investigating Office. The media will be ruthless in branding JS as a scamster, which is bound to affect FT. The easiest thing would be for me to move on. Almost everyone thinks that it would be the best alternative. I do not agree. Deep down, I feel JS has done no wrong. We are still gathering data to prove it. We have a good case. My conscience does not allow me to jump ship. What do you think?'

Mila went with my line of thinking. 'Do what you believe is right. Just take care. And yes, if there is a chance of you getting arrested, let me know in advance.'

That is all she said. I selected to stay on.

The result of the controversy was that FT, by the virtue of being in a regulated business, was compelled to exit all the exchanges that it owned or co-owned. FT's Board of Directors decided that the company would exit its various assets under protest.

As President I R M & A, who possessed capital market experience, the responsibility to accelerate the divestment was mine. Within twenty-four months, I concluded the divestment of seven assets to marquee names like Inter-Continental Exchange Group, USA (SMX), True North (NBHC), Kotak Mahindra Bank and RARE (MCX), Dalmia Bharat Ventures (IEX), DMCC (DGCX), RARE Enterprises and Edelweiss (MSEI) (among others), generating approximately Rs 3,000 crore in divestment as cash.

The surprise was not that the team was asked to engage in an activity for which it had not been recruited or for which it did not possess prior experience; the surprise (pleasant) was that the team that worked under unprecedented circumstances was rewarded commensurately by the Board.

For the first time, my conventional salary was replaced with a significant bonus; for the first time, relatively modest period inflows were substituted with a lumpy sum. Even as the company that I worked for was passing through its biggest challenge, my personal net worth was its largest. A large part of the corpus was immediately invested by me on the markets. The quantum almost tripled in three years.

Around Diwali 2014, a new reality emerged: there was a concerted demand for JS to step down as CEO and MD of FT. When JS read the writing on the wall, he recognized the need to hand over the visible leadership to someone who could interface with an independent Board of Directors on the one end and investors on the other; someone who could manage the business and treasury operations; someone who could be the public face of the company during the crisis.

He called me to his chamber one late afternoon. He said, 'I am recommending your name as my successor to the Board of Directors.'

That is how a 'Manager, Investor Relations' at Pantaloon Retail in 2003 became MD of one of the most dynamic exchange creators the world over in 2014 (Money Control, 2014).

Interestingly, Mila's fears came true. As CEO and MD of Financial Technologies, I received summons one day. I was to present myself to the Enforcement Directorate's office in Ballard Estate in Mumbai. At that time, JS was lodged in the Kalyan jail. The ED was attempting to rattle the FT team.

I told Mila, 'I was not in NSEL when the default transpired so I don't think I need to fear. But I am preparing you that there is a possibility that I could be arrested.'

She was scared. That was one of the few moments when I regretted staying on at FT. For the first time I asked myself in a quiet moment: 'Was my increased remuneration from FT worth *this*?'

I presented myself at the ED office at 11.00 a.m. on the appointed day. First surprise: I was not questioned until lunch. The post-lunch session was different. The ED mounted a one-way attack. I answered every question politely, kept defending myself as a professional only doing his job in the interest of FT shareholders. The ED threatened me with arrest. I told my interrogators that I was doing my duty within the guidelines of the law as CEO & MD. At 9.00 p.m., they recorded my statement, smiled and permitted me to leave. I was never summoned again.

When I stepped out and spoke to Mila on the mobile, I told her that it was usual and routine. It was a lie; when the officer mentioned the word 'arrest', the first vision that flashed past my mind was sitting in a corner behind bars next to JS.

In some months, after I had helped FT liquidate shareholding assets in other companies that could be monetized, the decisive take-home was that for a man who had invested no more than a few lakh in his business now possessed a clean Rs 2,000 crore in cash even after paying nearly Rs 1,000 crore of loans and after his business had been virtually wound up. It was a lesson validated: labour plus capital multiplied by risk-taking had translated into wealth.

There was another take-home: to not take advice from people you won't take criticism from. If I had listened to others, I would not have been CEO & MD and would also have lost self-respect for having deserted a sinking ship, and money.

The third lesson: life is unpredictable, so at best one needs to manage in a corridor of uncertainty. When I chose to stay at FT, little did I know that I would get the opportunity to manage complex cross-border deals worth Rs 3,000 crore with some of the most renowned global institutions. I got to sit on the boards of exchanges in Dubai, Singapore and Mauritius. Besides, my net worth increased substantially.

There was just one flipside. I had begun to believe that I could do virtually anything.

It was the germ of an arrogance that would one day warrant a vaccine.

6

Greed Is Good

Yeh dil maange more

When I was a child, my mother would wake my brother and me on Dhanteras, the first day of Diwali, to light diyas (small oil lamps) and write the words '*shubh laabh*' (auspicious profits) at the entrance to our home with *kanku* (red powder).

One day, I asked my uncle the meaning of the words. He said that in our Jain religion '*shubh*' meant goodness and '*laabh*' meant benefit. He interpreted it literally: '*Profit is good*'.

That brief exchange shaped my perception of money (and greed). My uncle added a critical disclaimer: 'Profit must be auspicious'.

The literal profit-is-good interpretation removed the burden of morality around money. Gradually, this seed took root: the greed to make money (extension of the profit-is-good philosophy) became integral to who I am.

41

This need began innocuously: as a means to provide for a better life where my friends at Neelkamal Building in Kolkata and cousins played catalysts. I saw their parents doing well, reflecting in what they wore, where they went for holidays; their homes were periodically renovated; the purchase of electronics (colour TVs and air-conditioners) and contemporary cars. Gradually, my *need* evolved into a *want*.

I desired more money to live the good life. I was a fifteen-year-old in the tenth standard when slot machines had been deployed in Kolkata. I pinched money from home and uncles' homes to gamble (which, when discovered, was treated with leniency by the family, partly because of the sympathy evoked by the loss of my father).

I wrestled with the concept of whether profit was *good*. This was partly the result of having been raised in a communist Bengal where the standard reaction to wealth accumulation was *'Aito taka niye ki korbi?'* (What will we do with all this money?)

The perception changed in 1989 when I was seventeen. I saw *Wall Street*, starring Michael Douglas as Gordon Gekko. He proclaimed, 'Greed, for lack of a better word, is good.' His argument: greed is a clean drive that 'captures the essence of the evolutionary spirit. Greed, in all of its forms – greed for life, for money, for love, for knowledge – has marked the upward surge of mankind.' That's it. Clarity.

Until then, I had perceived greed through the only lens I had possessed: the supposedly distorted. The pursuit of profit had been largely reviled. Greed has always been the hobgoblin of capitalism, the mischief it makes a canker on the faith of capitalists. It was conceded that it was immoral to be greedy. There was a selfishness of prefer-our-own-needs-over-those-of-the-people-around-us morality that came to be attached with greed. Anyone who devoted himself to the singular pursuit of money was dismissed even in our otherwise commerce-oriented Gujarati community as *'Paisa ni paachhar gaando thayi gayo chhey'* (He has gone mad chasing money).

Gordon Gekko parted the clouds. I began to see that greed lay at the heart of all progress. I could weave a difference between *greed* and *greedy*.

I began to get comfortable with the words 'You can be greedy and still feel good about yourself.'

My Tryst with Greed

I was twenty-two when my brother married.

Ironically, at a time when we needed to mobilize resources to host a decent marriage is when I came across the precious fuel for my greed.

When we extracted the share certificates that my late father had left behind and computed their overall value, we were surprised to discover that what we had once dismissed as meagre was not as insignificant as we had thought. The shares had multiplied 15x in fifteen years. My greed had needed a platform; it found one: the stock markets.

The stepping stones to the stock market comprised professional qualifications of chartered accountant and cost accountant. Few passed the CA and CWA final examinations in their maiden attempt. I cleared both in my first, studying while working eighteen hours a day across three years.

Greed was a good teacher. It created a sense of hunger. It enhanced focus. It encouraged perseverance. It incentivized discipline. The result: I excelled at work.

Greed taught me a big lesson: *that there is no such thing as a free lunch.* To become wealthy, one needed to take risks. The result is that by twenty-four, I started assuming risks larger than my net worth. I borrowed to trade and to invest. I bankrupted (almost) twice. I began to believe that I had come to appraise the risk–reward interplay.

Greed had an interesting spin-off. It created an obsession to make money fast. I didn't have time, I told myself. If I was to become wealthy by sixty-two, then that would be half a lifetime too late. I needed to succeed here and now. This obsession relocated me to Mumbai where I believed my persistence, professional education, experience, work ethic and risk-taking would be more completely rewarded.

In Mumbai, I assumed larger risks, acquired a home, purchased a fancy car, vacationed abroad, wore flashier clothes and watches, provided for a better family life and gained recognition. The best was yet to come. I was not just assuming risks with my money; I was also taking risks with opportunities. And they were working.

The irony is that even when a catastrophe materialized, I saw it as an opportunity.

At FT, even after the company encountered serious issues due to a payment default, I chose to stay on. A number of well-wishers felt this was a serious risk; my decision was vindicated professionally and financially as I almost single-handedly executed some of the most complex cross-border divestments of the company's assets to marquee names. I went on to become the CEO and MD with the biggest monetary bonus of my life. I saw greed and opportunity playing out well for me.

Greed wasn't just good; it was now in my DNA.

Because what happened thereafter – the other face of greed – became the story of my life.

From Greed to Greedy

Before I joined FT, my objective was to become wealthy.

Following the successful FT experience where my net worth multiplied 7x, my objective was to become *wealthier*.

I should have been satiated; instead, I became hungrier.

I should have told myself, 'Even a 7 per cent annual return on this corpus will leave me with remuneration far more than what I will be able to spend.' I should have told myself, 'This is the kind of sweet spot that most people dream of, where a sizeable liquid corpus keeps generating wealth for life.'

But I told myself: 'I need more.'

So when the FT crisis began to settle, I decided to make the next big move. My subconscious would still equate success in life to a wealth quantum. The image of Rakesh Jhunjhunwala's friends possessing net worth of hundreds of crores never left. Besides, the childhood perception of poverty kept returning. That vomiting after overeating, that refusal not to buy a Thums Up in Victoria, the Diwali pain were all still very much there in the subconscious.

I thought, *'Apna time aa gaya'* (My time has come). My net worth had manifolded. I had been raised from president to MD in minutes. I had started believing I was 'Amitabh Bachchan'. Whatever I touched would prove successful.

Kishore Biyani's words would keep coming back: 'Think big! The problem in India is that people think small.' I wanted to think big. Selfishly big. I didn't know why I wanted so much wealth, but I knew I just wanted it.

That is when a number began to float into my consciousness.

When I landed in Mumbai with Rs 3 lakh in my bank account, I had told myself that Rs 1 crore would be enough ('After that I will stop chasing money'). Thereafter, the target moved to Rs 3 crore ('After I get there, I will live life well'). The goalpost moved to Rs 10 crore ('What can one do in life without at least Rs 10 crore these days?').

So, when I had Rs 20 crore net worth on my books – a number I could have not contemplated at one time – even that began to appear miniscule. That number made me feel poorer. Nothing less than Rs 200 crore would convince me that I had indeed arrived and that I mattered in the world.

There was a realization that FT would no longer be the vehicle that would enable me to ten-fold my net worth. There was nothing to do there either.

I left FT.

Now that I was completely on my own, the big question was 'What next?'

I had the start in mind (existing net worth). I had the end in mind (Rs 200 crore).

All I now needed was the means – bigger and faster.

My search for a viable means to ten-fold my net worth in the shortest time drew me to the business models I had been exposed to during the preceding decade.

Future Group: Labour x Risk = Wealth

RARE: Capital x Risk = Wealth

FT: (Labour + Capital) x Risk = Wealth

Each of the visionary promoters had advocated that when you successfully fused capital, labour and risk-taking, what you got at the end of the day was a compelling valuation.

I began to apply each model to myself.

The RARE model would have been difficult for me since markets are inherently volatile; to use just capital as an active investor on the markets to reach Rs 200 crore in net worth warranted significant risk-taking, wide exposure to uncertainties and the heart of an ox.

If I fused labour with capital, I could have worked for a listed company and acquired a small stake within, which sounded well on paper, except that I didn't find anything exciting.

The only available option was the '(Labour + Capital) x Risk' model.

I saw myself as an entrepreneur with risk-taking capabilities.

The only challenge that remained: Finding a suitable venture.[*]

---

[*] Looking back can put things in perspective. On the one hand, Rs 20 crore would probably have been enough for me to last a lifetime given my lifestyle and everyday needs. And yet, I needed to achieve a number 10x that when my expenses would not have increased proportionately (or not increased at all). But then there are achievers like Mukesh Ambani, Kumar Mangalam Birla, Jeff Bezos, Bill Gates and Warren Buffett who continue to create more wealth. Why were they still in the race? Wasn't it time for them to say 'enough'? Perhaps their need to stay in the race was to leave a philanthropic legacy or be remembered as people who took their country to the top of the world or to invest in technology to solve the world's problems. In the end, wealth was a means to their life purpose. My case was different; I was interested in the obscenity of wealth, in other words, 'to show off'.

7

Health, Running and ...

Bhaag Milkha bhaag!

$\mathbf{M}$y childhood caught up with me in an unusual way in Mumbai.

One spin-off of a relatively deprived childhood in Kolkata was increased appetite (calorie in) offset with golf and cricket (calorie out).

This changed in Mumbai where the work was sedentary with no opportunity for sport. Eating out increased; a *vada pav* or *sev puri* (Mumbai street food) or roadside sandwich became a daily ritual; when travelling I was generally eating out; a large weekend feast with friends became usual.

My weight increased from 64 kg to 84 kg; a waist size of 32 inches became 38 inches.

I remembered what Anita Dongre (arising out of my experience of facilitating Future Group's investment in Anita

Dongre Fashions) had once told me: 'Prashant, it is none of my business but you need to lose weight badly. With every extra calorie that you give your body that it doesn't use, it turns into fat that is difficult to burn. Can you imagine how much pressure that puts on your heart?'

The mention of 'pressure on heart' was the trigger I needed. In usual circumstances I would have responded with a 'Yes, yes, will attend to it' procrastinated deferment; in my case, it served as an untimely alarm on account of my father's heart problem that went out of hand and interrupted a flourishing career. The picture of Arshia (my daughter) growing up without a father was a potent mental picture that made me reach for my mobile.

The following day I called Anita for help (she ran a health clinic in Bandra called 'Clay' where the now-famous dietician Pooja Makhija consulted). Pooja designed a diet plan. I meticulously followed her advice for four months. My weight declined to 67 kgs; the waist was back to 32 inches.

One of the mandatory things that Pooja included in her diet was walking for an hour. During these morning walks at the Juhu beach in Mumbai, I would come across a group of runners training for the Standard Chartered Mumbai Marathon. I joined and started training for half-marathons from 2013.

The more I ran, the more I realized that these runners were working professionals who invested in the best running gear. They would appraise soles. They would debate 'comfort'. They would dissect 'impact'.

The result is that each time I travelled abroad, I began to buy a couple of pairs of new running shoes that had passed the approval of the running group (at one point I had nearly twenty pairs of virtually any brand one can think of).

Most runners found running shoes expensive. A typical running shoe lasted about 500–600 km, the distance we ran in about four months, by which time the cushion began to wear off and exposed the runners to probable injury. A decent pair of running shoes (Nike, Asics, Adidas, Puma, etc.) retailed between Rs 10,000 and Rs 15,000. For successful working professionals this may not have been a high price tag but for one detail: they needed to change their shoes every few months. Besides, they needed to invest in shorts, T-shirts, events, gymnasium training and travel to events. The result is that during any year, I would spend more than Rs 1,50,000 on just running, travel not included (the irony being that a premium sport like golf was probably only half as expensive).

When the runners did not want to buy expensive running shoe global brands, the next available choice (Indian) would be priced at around Rs 2,000 but not provide the technology to bear the body impact of a runner across 21/42 kilometres (estimated at 3x body weight).

There was nothing decent in between.

Then one day it struck me. There were thousands of runners across India like me. They didn't wish to spend Rs 15,000 for a pair of shoes; they didn't want the low-cost-low-quality option for Rs 2,000. They wanted something that combined elements of both – affordable quality. My brain started recognizing patterns and making visual connections. I sensed untapped potential. The white space began to emerge.

I visited Nike, Adidas, Reebok, Puma and Skechers outlets, and engagements with their staff over the next few weeks widened my perspective: why some shoes were priced 2x; why the sole of one was thicker; what material had been used in most; which company priced at a premium.

Each time I lifted the shoe tongue to see where it had been manufactured only two names emerged: China and Vietnam. China was initially the world manufacturing capital, but as labour costs increased, the sports shoe manufacturing industry began to shift to Vietnam where it enjoyed the advantages of labour cost and modern equipment.

By now I had begun to get interested enough to get deeper into the subject. My mind would not like the idea of an 'open loop'. I needed answers.

It was one click on my laptop that transformed my life.

8

The Lucky Discovery

Khul ja sim sim

After I left FT and had no job, I would leave home to 'work' from Starbucks in Juhu, Mumbai.

I would spend three hours there from 9.30 a.m., return for lunch, conduct a few calls, or step out to meet people.

I remember that day in particular. I opened my Microsoft Surface, sipped my triple-shot Americano and googled 'Chinese sports shoe brands'. A waterfall of information cascaded. From the top ten, I selected ANTA. The moment I clicked, I was directed to anta.cn.

I cannot describe what I discovered: I was like a child in a candy store. I did not know then that ANTA was China's biggest sports footwear and apparel brand. I had not even heard of them. First the look of the shoes (attractive). Next the range of the shoes (extensive, screen after screen). Then the price (between

RMB 150 and 400, or Rs 1,500–4,000). Then the categories (running, basketball, casual, sneakers, soccer and so on). And finally the proprietary technology.

ANTA was like any global sports brand: endorsed by brand ambassadors from within China as well as US basketball and boxing icons. And the amazing thing is that here I hadn't even heard of ANTA; no marathoner from our group had even mentioned it. My curiosity provoked, I googled 'anta + market capitalization'. The number I found was USD 12 billion or Rs 90,000 crore. *Bloody hell*, I hissed. I downloaded ANTA's investor presentation and annual report. The brand that the company owned was ANTA (lower end). The brands it represented in China comprised FILA (mid-end) and Descente (premium). The company generated revenues of Rs 35,000 crore and profit before tax of Rs 4,500 crore (2017). In twenty years, ANTA had opened over 10,000 stores in China (ANTA, 2021).

ANTA was not alone. China had other brands like Li Ning, X-Step, Peak, Diadora, 361 and more. They marketed products to a middle-income China seeking to buy shoes in the Rs 1,500–4,000 (RMB 150–400) market … through 45,000+ stores.

At one level, one was disappointed that despite possessing a population of more than 1.3 billion people, India did not have a single affordable home-grown sports brand; besides, the number of retail stores in India were a fraction of China.

At another level, one was excited. If one could create a company equivalent to just 5 per cent of ANTA in ten years, that would still be 500 stores, which would have been almost the retail footprint of Adidas India or Nike India in 2017.

Five hundred stores. I rolled that number on my tongue. Started with back-of-the-envelope calculations on my laptop. Assuming revenue throughput of Rs 2 crore per store per annum in the tenth year with an equivalent throughput being generated from online, multi-brand outlets and traditional distribution segments, one would have created a company generating ~Rs 2,000 crore in revenues. If a 3x price-to-revenue multiple were to be applied, the company could be potentially valued at Rs 6,000 crore. If I owned even a third of the business at that point, the value of my holding would be worth Rs 2,000 crore.

I froze.

That night while I tossed and turned in bed, a voice began to whisper: 'Your Rs 20 crore in the bank in 2017 could become Rs 2,000 crore by 2027.'

The next morning, I journalized: Rs 20 crore to Rs 2,000 crore in 10 years.

Underlined for impact.

I had my start line and my finish fine. A new life journey had commenced.

The words of Paulo Coelho from *The Alchemist* – 'And, when you want something, all the universe conspires in helping you to achieve it' – began to come back to me (Shah Rukh Khan articulated these words on the film screen – *'Kehte hain agar kisi cheez ko dil se chaaho ... toh puri qaayanaat usse tumse milaane ki koshish mein lag jaati hai'*.

THE DARE

9

Becoming an Entrepreneur

Badhe chalo!

Obsession. The feeling when something emerges from the periphery of one's consciousness and assumes monopoly?

The feeling when an internal voice orders one forward with the words 'Not a minute to lose; your destiny awaits you'.

This is what happened to me when the prospect of transforming Rs 20 crore into Rs 2,000 crore across ten years began to occupy my consciousness.

I saw in that the germ of new possibilities.

Where Indians would want to buy my products not only because they were priced honestly but because what I was offering represented the first truly Indian sports brand.

Where grateful consumers would tell me, 'We always wanted to buy an Indian sports brand. You finally made it affordable, accessible and attractive.'

Where prospective distributors would call for my brand and one would have to turn them away with the words, 'We don't have enough stocks, sorry!'

Where private equity firms sought to buy into our business and our standard reply would be 'We don't need money currently; we are planning an IPO.'

Where ANTA and Nike would dispatch representatives to discuss prospects of a collaboration or a buyout.

The result of this obsessive ferment was urgency. The need to do everything *now*. The need to advance business development. The need to have a number of priorities in concurrent movement. The need to establish a company. The need to recruit partners and employees. The need to market this undiscovered story to prospective investors.

There was no time to dither.

The big goal of growing my wealth to Rs 2,000 crore in ten years had been established.

There was something serving as the tail wind to this ambition.

In India, fitness was becoming mainstream. A number of sportsmen were advocating fitness and healthy eating. People read of Virat Kohli's fitness obsession and dreamt, *I want to be fit like him*. Six-pack abs and hourglass figures were in. A new gym look was making heads turn on social media.

The Slip between the Cup and the Lip

The big picture was promising. The fine print, not so. Though I could dream about the what, I struggled with the how. I had always been a finance professional. Though I knew what to look for in a sports shoe (being a runner), I had no clue about how to make one or source one.

I shared this opportunity with my running friends. Gradually their excitement would wear thin when I would tell them about my dilemma. One friend told me to visit Alibaba.com. He said I would be surprised.

The Eureka Moment

The gateway to my aspiration to create something unique in India was China, more specifically Alibaba.com. Being a listed company, I was aware of Alibaba and its business model. One merely needed to type 'running shoes' and 36,000+ searches would flash past. Alibaba.com was in a different orbit compared with IndiaMART or the Just Dial app in India; Alibaba.com didn't just provide the name and address of a sports shoe manufacturer; since it had recognized that buyers worldwide would think twice before trusting a Chinese brand that they had never before used, it provided comfort-enhancing assurances: Alibaba's rating of that manufacturer's capabilities based on a multi-year track record, Alibaba's trade assurance, Alibaba's insurance (which meant that if one was dissatisfied with the product or service then one was not obliged to pay), a listing of the number of years that the company had been selling on Alibaba, the outsourcing partner's response rate to queries and the number of successful transactions having been concluded.

I spent a week browsing the catalogue of fifty-odd manufacturers on Alibaba.com. My reference point would always be ANTA and its price points. I liked most of what I saw. The products appeared similar to ANTA's; besides, the pricing on the catalogues (when converted into Indian currency) appeared affordable. A ray of hope was emerging.

Alibaba was not just listing running shoe manufacturers; it was facilitating direct interface with manufacturers. I called to establish a connect; the voice at the other end answered in

English (surprise). I explained what I was trying to do in India; the voice appeared friendly and willing to help.

The one thing the various voices suggested: come and visit us at the Canton Fair in Guangzhou in May (less than a month away). Before Alibaba.com entered my world, I had been directionless; after that productive week, I was hopeful.

I called my childhood friend Samir. 'China *chalega?*' (Want to visit China?) I asked. The result was that tickets were booked, hotels identified, visas applied for and Canton Fair registration completed.

Canton Fair.

Whatever one may have heard about its size, the first sight of the spatial spread of this event takes time to digest. Samir and I did not exchange a word. We ogled. The area of the shoe and sports apparel section alone at the Fair (part of Phase 3) was larger than … larger than the Wankhede Stadium in Mumbai.

Spread across 50,000 square feet were manufacturers and manufacturers. Showcasing shoes of leather, canvas, formal, casual, men, women, kids, toddlers, construction, skiing, sandals, chappals, flipflops… sport. Plus, every size, every colour, every price point, every technology and every possible combination.

I had come from scratch to the Disneyworld of sports shoes.

At every stall Samir and I visited, we would physically examine the bend of the shoe from toe to heel. We would examine the shoe from outsole to upper. We would feel the fabric texture between the thumb and index finger. We would wear to see if they provided walking comfort. We would turn to each other and say, 'Just the kind of sports shoes we need in India.'

In the space of those five days, Samir and I covered nearly 200 stalls. We took pictures of the shoes we liked. We noted the minimum orders required to place orders. We noted the free-onboard (FOB) price for every shoe. We collected visiting cards. It was interesting to see several Indians. We even chatted with a few in our hotel.

At our Fraser Suites hotel in Guangzhou, Samir and I would compare the pictures we clicked to arrive at a pricing visibility: even after adding the import duty and marking 3x–4x up (retailer's mark-up), the price would still be in the affordable Rs 2,500–3,500 range. This was precisely the price band within which ANTA was retailing products, so things began to fall in place. We began to shortlist manufacturers who fitted our composite vision of quality, design, minimum order quantity and price.

When Samir and I had started for Canton Fair, we knew that if the event had not delivered, it would have been the end of my dream. As things stood at the end of the last day at Canton Fair, we faced the other problem – a bewildering range of options to select from.

We walked out of the Canton Fair a couple of inches off the ground. We hadn't just arrived at breakthrough costing; we had made a product discovery. We could have flown back to India with our mission complete; instead, we decided to visit shortlisted manufacturers. This could have created a second round of logistical planning but for an interesting detail: virtually all the manufacturers were in one Chinese city (Jinjiang) that was an hour's flight from Guangzhou.

On the last day, when we started seeking appointments with the shortlisted Jinjiang manufacturers, we were surprised. Each one asked us for the date, which hotel we would be staying in and our preferred time of visit. They weren't just being courteous; at the appointed hour their car would arrive at our hotel to collect us. The warmth of their engagement, the extent of their interest in our presence at their facility – without due diligence of our seriousness, seniority, or liquidity – came as a surprise. They were going all out to send us a message that they valued our business.

Curiously, we encountered the problem of plenty. Samir and I prospected twenty-one manufacturing facilities in seven days. We ordered 100+ sample pairs of shoes to test in India. We were confused about which manufacturer to work with.

In a quiet moment I began to wonder: how had the rest of India missed such an evident sourcing opportunity?

THE DETERMINATION
(18 MONTHS)

10

Know Your Customer

Main hoon na

My engagement with Kishore Biyani was one of my more enriching experiences.

He had mapped the Pantaloons/Central/Big Bazaar consumer to be able to predict what he or she would buy given his/her income. He would travel economy class to observe what his target audience would be wearing. He would examine colours, apparel, bags and shoes, drawing up a mental index of what those people would be earning, what kind of homes they would be living in, what kind of surpluses they would be generating and what they would be likely to spend on. He could ease into the shoes of consumers and think like them. Never was he arrogant enough to think 'I am my own consumer, so I know best.'

All these observations went into the melting pot of his mind where he arrived at a simple understanding: at what price would he be able to sell what product, in what quantity, in which region and at what juncture.

I observed Kishore Biyani closely enough for years to tell myself that I understood that 'software'.

So, while engaged in the pursuit of launching an honest Indian sports brand, I felt, I knew who my real consumer was. People like me, that is.

People compelled to buy a Nike or an Adidas at a five-figure sticker price because an alternative pair that met the mid-market consumer's requirement was not available.

People like me who ran with a purpose in an India becoming increasingly conscious of health, fitness and wellness.

People like me who took pride in everything Indian.

So, every question that I would have asked a potential customer in a random sample survey, I asked myself: 'Would you, Prashant Desai, have brought a sports shoe for Rs 3,000 that was not as large a brand as a German or American icon but priced a third of that?'

'Would you, Prashant Desai, have brought a sports shoe positioned as the Next Big Indian Thing serving a market ignored by German or American brands?'

'Would you, Prashant Desai, believe there are thousands of Indian consumers like you who will be keen to buy into a new sports shoe and apparel brand?'

The answer in each case: 'Yes.'

This was an India comprising people like me. People who had grown from middle-income families. People who aspired for the better. People who felt a deeper national pride to buy things Indian and world-class.

The time had come.

I didn't need to validate my conviction with anyone to appraise whether I was headed in the right direction. Those I had spoken to had been captivated by the passion of my argument. Besides,

Samir, whom I had taken with me on this reconnaissance (not from the shoe business), had been sucked into the excitement. This was going to be big, he had said.

Ironically, the contrarian was Kishore Biyani himself. I met him on the opening of their FBB store in Kolkata and relayed this thought to get his feedback, *'Ek baar aur soch lo'* (think once more), he said. 'I have done this sports shoe business in the past. It is not as simple as it appears. The power of global brands is large, and the Indian consumer is just not discerning enough.'

I had a ready answer for this (for myself, not him). Kishore Biyani was talking of a 2010 experience in 2017. He had done this business years ago when the Indian consumer was still maturing. The fitness revolution was then only picking up. Disposable incomes were not as high then as they were now.

Besides, Kishore Biyani didn't run. He didn't know the actual user; I did.

As a concession, I felt that if he had ventured into marketing sports shoes at this point – the way I was – he would have made a success of it.

'The time is right,' I said to myself, 'to prove Kishore Biyani wrong.'

What Others Said

One of the first things I did was to test my hypothesis.

I showed the samples to my running friends. Their first reaction was a wow. They liked the colours, feel, technology and presentability. There was something else they said that sounded credible; they wouldn't wear the shoes for the main events or long runs but would surely do so for practice runs.

Next on the list was Vinod Naidu, who had managed Sachin Tendulkar's endorsement and business interests for more than a decade-and-a-half and was arguably India's best sports marketing professional. Then on the list was Rajiv Mehta, credited to have built Puma India from scratch into an ~Rs 800 crore annual revenues company in under nine years. The next was Sanjeev Agrawal, my ex-colleague at Future Group and former MD and CEO of Skechers India (by then the fastest growing sports shoes brand in India).

I ran my marketing spiel with each: why India needed a world-class affordable sports shoe like ANTA that would be made for India by Indians; how there was a middle-market gap that needed to be plugged and how I had a product that would be affordable, attractive, available and accessible. Finally.

I showed the samples that I had brought from China. 'Just Rs 3,000 for this,' I would say as slowly as I could to maximize impact.

I met Vinod first at the Trident at BKC, Mumbai. Vinod got so excited by the time I had got to half my spiel that he wanted to be in on the business with me and whipped out his phone to call the legendary Indian cricketer and then the coach of Indian cricket team, Anil Kumble (who was a few rooms away at the same hotel), with these words: 'I really think you should see this. Come right away!' Anil Kumble was then the coach of the Indian cricket team. Through his sporting career he had seen and used several big brands. He looked at the shoes and apparel closely. He tried them on. He even went and brought his sports gear that he was using. I was nervous. He asked a few questions. And then Anil Kumble pronounced the verdict of 'Nine on ten', and said something else that made me smile on the drive back home as if I had discovered a 100-bagger (when a stock goes up 100x): 'How can I get associated?'

Rajiv's opinion I would value the most. The man was an achiever in the world of sports brands. Managing director of Puma India by twenty-seven. Understood brand building.

Understood India. Understood the consumer. Understood prices and demand. Understood where lifestyle aspirations were headed. Understood retail, distribution and online marketing. He too concurred. India was a country of 1.3 billion consumers and there was not a single sports shoe brand in excess of Rs 1,500 crore in annual revenues. Crazy. His words when he saw the shoe I presented in Bengaluru: 'Looks interesting. Product *ma dum chhey*' (The product has potential).

I was yet to hear a negative. Gradually, my guarded optimism was to turn into full-blown confidence. When I entered J.W. Marriott, Juhu, to meet my third screening filter, Sanjeev Agrawal, I was walking an inch above the ground.

Sanjeev red-flagged me. 'It's not as easy as you think,' he said. KB (Kishore Biyani) had prospected the same business a few years ago with all its brand building, product understanding, retail network and procurement capabilities – and failed, he said. Sanjeev kept provoking: 'Why should I buy your shoe for Rs 3,000 when I could buy an end-of-season sale Nike/Adidas/Skechers/Puma for Rs 3,000 as well? Besides, *yeh designs aur colours vaahiyaat hain* (your designs and colours are ridiculous). Why would anyone want to buy a pink sports shoe? Only black, blue and grey sell!'

I countered that this was precisely the mental block we were fighting. Normal was boring; this was an India seeking to stand out. Sanjeev kept parrying: 'You have not done your research of what sells and does not sell. Go to Reliance Footprint or Big Bazaar or even the mom-and-pop stores in Parel East or the Dadar market. You will get your answers.'

I quoted the Great Biyani: 'Don't overdo research. Shelf test is better than self-test.' Sanjeev countered, '*Bhai* (Brother), do you have his capital and risk appetite?' Finally, I put this down to the embedded Devil's Advocate in him not wishing or willing to see that I had a potential winner. Before Sanjeev left, he told me, 'I will be happy to help. Keep meeting for friendly unpaid advice once a month. And yes, Prashant, *ek baar market me jaao phir se. Yeh duniya alag nazariye se bhi dekho. Itna easy nahin hai sab'* (Go and visit the market once more, see this world through a different lens too. It is not so easy.)

I never met Sanjeev again.

Is there really a comparable player?

A view similar to Sanjeev's was expressed by Santosh Desai much later when I met him to help position the brand.

Santosh was considered a marketing guru who had helped position brands like Titan, Colgate, Royal Enfield, Kellogg's, Pepsi, Lenskraft and others. Santosh was my colleague at Future Group, heading Future Brands for Kishore ji.

Santosh possessed the capacity to listen to a client's story for days and emerge with a unique take on the brand's personality (and positioning).

Santosh would help enhance clarity on how the product needed to be positioned, what communication would work with consumers and create the foundation for a successful launch.

Santosh and his team heard my practised spiel. That in the sports shoe pyramid in India there were Nike and Adidas at the apex, there were commodity products at the bottom, but when it came to buying a sports shoe brand – attractive, trendy, mid-priced and fundamentally Indian – around Rs 3,000, the space was largely empty. I narrated the disproportionate growth in the same category in China in general and ANTA in particular. 'There is a gap just like in China in the Indian mid-priced sports shoe category,' I said, 'and we have a product that is differentiated enough to fill it.'

Curiously, we had come to Santosh without being able to show him the product since it was still under development.

Based on the concept, we needed Santosh and his team to craft the personality of the brand.

Surprisingly, after a fortnight's research, Santosh and team said no. Not to the assignment. They said no to our assumptions.

One. 'The vast gap around Rs 3,000 is fiction. All you need to do is get on to Myntra or Amazon and you will find several sports shoe options priced below Rs 3,000.'

Two. 'You are not seeing the market gap, product and brand from the consumer's perspective.'

And yet, Santosh and his team said something more. That the story had some merit. What they also saw in India were products, products and products. No brands. There was indeed the opportunity and gap to build a truly Indian sports brand in that space.

One of the first things I did after engaging with Santosh and his team was order several sporty shoes around the sub-Rs 3,000 level from Myntra and Amazon with the objective to stack them product to product and compare with our sample (at least what I had in mind of our product).

I used four parameters.

First, the look and the finish of the shoes. Did they look as attractive compared to a Nike or an Adidas? If I removed their logo and replaced it with a Nike or Adidas logo, would they 'belong'?

Ours was good-looking and original.

Second, how did they fit? How did they feel on wearing? Were they comfortable? Did all the shoes from the same brand have a similar fit? Did they work on the last?

All our shoes had the same fit, like a denim from the same brand. We had developed an original last.

Third, did the shoes have any technology to speak of? What material did they use?

There was no technology to speak of. We had, however, invested in original moulds.

Fourth, how did they stack up on the price versus value matrix? Would one buy because they were cheap or because at that price they offered substantial value?

They fared well on price, period. But there was no value proposition like ours.

Following this scrutiny, our conviction hardened.

I came to a conclusion: Santosh may be right on options and price, but he was comparing apples with oranges. He needed to compare us with the Adidases of the world and not the generic sports shoes discounting themselves as commodities on Amazon and Myntra.

He wasn't seeing what I was seeing; he would soon come around, I concluded.

11

The Partnership

Rab ne bana di jodi

June 2017.

It was time to build a leadership team.

I fell back on Rajiv Mehta, who I had known for some time. Rajiv possessed impressive credentials; he had been MD and CEO of Puma India. More than that, Rajiv was now a brand in his own right, having grown Puma from scratch into a business that generated Rs 800 crore in annual revenues by the time he left.

Following my return from the Canton Fair, I engaged with him on occasions, posing questions on how I should proceed. Rajiv had moved from Puma to Arvind. By the time I was speaking to him, he had left Arvind and was contemplating his next move.

I seized this lull in his career to ask if he could become the CEO of my venture. The brief: he needed to merely replicate what he had accomplished at Puma: even if he proved half as successful, he – and we – would become fabulously wealthy.

I proposed a number. This is how I presented my math: when we achieve Rs 200 crore in revenues at the end of the fifth year and were valued at no more than one-time revenue (worst case scenario), his 15 per cent sweat equity would be worth Rs 30 crore.

Rajiv played the idea in his mind. His father had worked in Wipro; each time the father had generated a job surplus, he would invest in the company's stock. The result was that when Wipro extended from the edible oils business to information technology, the petty investments transformed into family silver.

D:FY could be Rajiv's Wipro.

A few days later, Rajiv called. He wanted to meet; he flew down from Bengaluru to Mumbai. He said, 'I liked what you had to say but didn't also completely like what you had to say.' The bottom line: 'I don't wish to be an employee. I wish to bear equal risk. I want to be equal partner,' he said.

I remember what I did a few minutes later. I excused myself and walked to the rest room at the J.W. Marriott, Juhu, where we met. Once the door had closed and I had ensured there was no one there, I punched my fist in the air and shouted 'Yesssssss!' Almost like I had won at Wimbledon.

Rajiv would later share his reasons for coming in as a partner. Assuming we were successful (Rs 200 crore revenues in five years), he felt we would get a 3x price-to-revenue valuation. That number made sense to him. In the past, he had demonstrated his credentials, but the upside was largely carved away by the employer (Puma). This time round he would be working for himself.

The result was that Rajiv wasn't just willing to bring his experience and capability to the table. He was willing to put his skin into the game with an investment equal to mine (we eventually settled at 60:40 in my favour).

This had a curious fallout. My budget for a decent launch had been around Rs 10 crore, but with Rajiv's entry, there were options: keep the launch outlay constant, reduce my personal outflow and keep some money in reserve for a prospective top-up, or draw immediately on his contribution and increase the outlay towards Rs 20 crore.

We doubled. Doubled everything in fact. The cash. The talent. The risks.

I justified this on the grounds that this adequate corpus would separate us from the other start-ups who would start with low cash, would raise funds prematurely and dilute precious equity at a low valuation. With Rs 20 crore as seed capital – not many start-ups in India start out with as large a capital outlay – we would be able to resist the temptation of raising angel or seed capital but proceed towards Series A (reward ahead of risk).

The game had been graduated to an effective launch pad. From here it could only get bigger.

I banked on Rajiv to deliver the Puma magic in our start-up company. I told myself, 'This man has done what few CEOs of sports product companies in India have achieved. If he says that one should only gun for a quarter of what he achieved at Puma across the first five years at our company then at least he is being honest.'

There was an awe that Rajiv brought to our table.

On one instance, my back-of-the-envelope calculation indicated that one needed to market 35,000 sports shoes in the first six months (based on a minimum quote by China) – 200 pairs per day. To me, this appeared relatively easy; we would be marketing to a population of 1.36 billion and worrying about selling 200 pairs a day. That number one could be selling in

Mumbai alone, I felt. I thought we would fall short. I asked him. Rajiv said 'It is more than enough. We will not be able to sell 35,000 but it is fine as we will need some inventory from the first season to carry into the next.'

I asked why that was important. Rajiv said that revenues were a function of customer choice. The wider the choice (and inventory), the higher the revenues. At that time, we nursed an inventory of about 35 SKUs; Puma had over 120. For a new brand perhaps 35 would be a good starting number, Rajiv added; we could carry this to the second season when we added another 35 SKUs and have 70 SKUs on offer, which would be presentable.

Based on mutual respect, we did not segregate our responsibilities: both would address retail, online sales, operations, finance, marketing, HR and execution. There was a reason for being relatively unstructured: there was a mutual understanding that as challenges emerged, we would adapt. Since Rajiv and I were co-founders, each would gravitate to his subject of interest and we would share specific responsibilities as things progressed.

When two individuals set out to become partners, the most critical challenge is the ability to get along as people and professionals.

I believed that we possessed the right complement: Rajiv possessed a first-hand understanding of how sports shoes are sold in India; I came with a hands-on understanding of finance, capital mobilization and ability to see the big picture. I considered Rajiv to be the 'elder brother' when it came to sales and execution led by retail; I felt I was the 'older brother' when it came to strategy, expansion, brand positioning and financial management. Besides, both had worked in large, layered and multi-segment systems-driven companies.

This typically Indian 'elder brother' syndrome was the beginning of the confusion: I chose to treat Rajiv as family and not as a professional. This dilemma surfaced when he said he intended to sell his BMW. He needed cash flows to sustain his standard of living since we had agreed to sacrifice salaries for the first three years of the company's existence until we had generated adequate surpluses.

Instead of letting this development be treated with commensurate empathy, I began to emotionalize: 'What if this had been my brother, Ketan? What would have been my response?' Rather than be a dispassionate bystander, I pitched in. 'I don't want you to compromise your lifestyle,' I said. I told Rajiv not to sell his BMW and that we would figure something out. After all, he was 'family'.

We worked out an arrangement: Rajiv would draw a salary from the business (that would be set off against his next equity infusion). Now it was Rajiv's turn to return the gesture. He suggested that I take a salary as well. I was touched that he was concerned about my welfare. I don't remember the exact words with which I responded but I told him that if anything ever happened to him, his children would be 'my responsibility'.

The professional was fusing with the personal. The personal was getting kind of mushy.

And we were far from selling our first shoe.

12

The Product Obsession

Ji jaan se

July 2017.

Rakesh Jhunjhunwala, one of India's most successful investors, explained his most effective stock-picking filter: 'The attractiveness of the addressable opportunity, a sustainable competitive advantage, scalability and operating leverage. This cocktail generates a multi-bagger (a stock that multiplies in value).'

His words had been carefully selected: he didn't say exciting market; he used the words 'attractive' and 'addressable'. He didn't just use the words 'competitive advantage'; he added 'sustainable'. Both these were critical for scale (growth) and profits (operating leverage) and eventually for valuation.

This learning stayed. I knew that a large addressable market existed for a truly Indian sports brand addressing the vast and growing Indian mid-income class. As per capita growth incomes grew in India, so would the spending on fitness. The moment the consumer spent on sport or fitness – outdoor sport or indoor gymnasium – it was inevitable that he or she would need to buy sports gear. There was a correlation: fitness meant sports gear.

Now come to the 'sustainable competitive advantage' part. My introduction to the wide range of what China had to offer was the first step towards creating that advantage. Buying a ticket to China, attending to the Canton Fair and then connecting to Jinjiang was no advantage in itself; anyone could have done that. However, the competitive advantage lay in being able to appraise the vast merchandise on offer and know precisely what combination of products and colours would represent an effective season's offerings. The trick lay in being able to decode what combination – colours, sizes, styles and embedded technology – would be right for a contemporizing India at what price.

Assuming that this merchandizing insight – of what to buy for a modernizing and aspiring India – represented a competitive advantage, was it sustainable? I felt it would prove to be. If one kept going back to China to examine the range it had to offer and kept connecting the dots backwards to how the consumer in India was evolving, then the advantage would not be one-time, it would be sustainable. The deeper one explored in both countries, the wider one's knowledge would get and the more effective one would be. If that was not sustainable, what was? And then there were investments which no other Indian sports brand was doing the way we envisaged.

There was one other point that addressed sustainability. The Adidases of the world had invested millions of dollars in technology, which represented a superior understanding of the biomechanics, the kinetic chain of running, the impact of one on the other and ways of mitigating runner impact. As someone entering the same business, I could not overlook the subject of technology. It was something that every consumer would eventually have considered anyway: will this sports shoe protect my feet, knees and back?

We gradually discovered what we thought was our answer: we didn't need to invest as much as the Adidases of the world because the market segment they addressed was not my addressable audience. If someone was open to spending Rs 12,000 for a high-end pair of sports shoes, then he or she was not my consumer. The price-sensitive consumer was the one we prospected: someone who did not wish to spend more than Rs 3,000 a pair. The segregation was clear: those who sought cutting-edge technology would do well to prospect marquee brands at a higher price; those who could do with something that had been reverse-engineered would buy at our price point. Besides, we assumed that the Indian consumer would be discerning enough to understand the difference between a Nike and our product, the basis of our 'sustainable' competitive advantage. We decided to go ahead by sourcing an off-the-shelf midsole and outsole design and technology from China.

It is here that we believed we possessed a prudent balance: validated technology (I would not agree to the word 'outdated') that would be marketed well; product priced considerably lower than today's technology and eminently affordable. The answer was blowing in the wind: millions of price-sensitive Indians would prefer the lower-priced alternative because this is precisely what they had been doing through their lives: resisting the expensive and selecting the honestly priced.

If consumers would begin to tire of the midsole or outsole technology and design we had to offer, we could always fly back to China and buy something that had succeeded a few years ago, repeating the entire cycle. This then would be our 'sustainable competitive advantage'.

This premise came from the gut feeling that the Indian consumer would not be picky about 'technology' in sports shoes, especially when they had been priced at Rs 3,000 or so. This rationale had been showcased in India's mobile handset market where for every Apple or Samsung smartphone there was also an Oppo, Vivo, Xiaomi and Redmi. The consumer was no fool; she was discerning enough to know that she was not getting an iPhone experience while buying an Oppo or a Vivo when she was buying at a fraction of the iPhone sticker price.

The same rationale then would apply to our sports shoe proposition.

Truly Indian, Truly Original

Rajiv and I agreed on one thing: we would not invest in serious sports shoe technology.

To compensate, we would outsource breathtakingly attractive products. This could prove to be a competitive advantage: the Nikes and Adidases could continue to market technology-intensive sports shoes. We would offer sports shoes that consumers would like to flaunt on Instagram, Facebook and Snapchat. We would create a brand that would be easily selling the best-looking sports shoes at Rs 3,000.

So, when our first round of ordered samples arrived from China, the conclusion was 'decent', 'reasonable' and 'fairly okay.' No one said, 'I want this.'

The reason was that these sports shoes had been crafted around designs copied from global brands. Those global brands had been in the market for some time. There was no 'never seen this before' halo around them.

We agreed on the second thing: if we were to create a truly Indian sports brand, the shoes would not be copies of an original. They would be original. This validated what I had experienced in stores: customers preferring an attractive shoe over a technology-rich equivalent.

The result was that we were beginning to arrive at our first sustainable competitively advantaged product configuration: design-heavy but technology-light coupled with differentiated branding.

The immediate endeavour was to seek sports shoe designers. Our experience within India was disappointing; a country of more than 1.3 billion people did not have a single competent sport shoes designer (partly because no Indian sports shoes brand went design-first, we told ourselves).

First Sustainable Competitive Advantage: Original Design

An extensive Internet search (LinkedIn and Google) took me to the capital of sports shoes designers in the world: Portland, Oregon, USA (twenty minutes from Nike World headquarters in Beaverton, Oregon). If China was the manufacturing capital of sports shoes, Portland was its design hub. Ever since Phil Knight launched a running shoe in the 1960s in that location off the US West Coast and transformed his company into a generic name for sports shoes (Nike), Portland transformed: it didn't quite become a city marked by a large number of manufacturing facilities as much as it became a designer's mecca. An entire community of sports shoe designers emerged: someone who had worked with Nike turned independent; someone who had worked for Nike's competitor set up a design studio; the result was that if you needed to design a world-class sports shoe, you went to Portland, period.

We too prospected sports shoe designers in Portland. We explored LinkedIn and soon we were speaking to select designers (keener to send us an invoice for $10,000 than say 'Can we hear your story first?'). We came across Pensole, perhaps the only sports shoe design school in the world. The founder, D'Wayne Edwards, excused himself on the grounds that his fees would be unaffordable for us (but made up for blunt speak by connecting us to Miroslav Milanov, who had previously worked with New Balance and Keen, which was as good as canvassing for competition).

Miroslav and Jeremy

Passionate sports shoe design professionals. Not the usual 'In what name do we send our bill?', but more of the 'Tell us why you need to make this shoe and we will take it from there.' Rather than doing this over Skype, we decided to visit them in Portland.

I flew over. Portland is Oregon's largest city. The city is quaint with the river Willamette flowing north through downtown Portland. Portland is famous for its love affair with food, coffee and beer. It has 600 street food carts and most microbreweries in the world and is a leader in speciality coffee. Nike is headquartered twenty minutes from downtown Portland; Adidas's North American headquarters and design centre are based there. Pensole, the world's only footwear design academy, is there too.

The first morning after I landed, I went for a run. I saw runners all around. Like most countries where I have run, runners were friendly. I joined a runner and ran along the river with him. Over coffee later, he said, thanks to Nike and Adidas, running is popular in Portland. Every year, the city hosts the Portland Marathon as well as parts of the Hood to Coast Relay, the world's largest long-distance relay race (by number of participants). Portland also serves as the centre to an elite running group, the Nike Oregon Project, and is the residence of several elite runners including the British 2012 Olympic 10,000 metre and 5,000 metre champion Mo Farah, American record holder at 10,000 metre Galen Rupp and 2008 American Olympic bronze medallist at 10,000 metre Shalane Flanagan.

As a runner, I was besotted.

I met Miro and Jeremy at Hotel Crown Plaza overlooking the Willamette river. Both were young and warm as they shook my hand. They welcomed me and we sat at the coffee shop. They wanted to understand in detail my vision. I took them through the opportunity for a mid-priced truly Indian sports brand. I told them about my running. India's growing economy. The sedentary lifestyles. The need to make a faithful Indian sports shoe for the bulge of the country's population. The social media obsession. The Canton Fair visit. The samples. And finally, our differentiator of breathtakingly good-looking original-design shoes.

Miroslav and Jeremy prodded, 'What is your portfolio going to be like? How many options are you planning to launch in the first season? Of these how many do you want designed as originals?'

I gathered a response that would mask my confusion: 'Three to four originals and around five or six off-the-shelf copies from China,' I said with an air as if I knew the subject after years of market prospecting. 'There will be everything for everyone,' I added sagely.

Miro was the first to shake his head. 'Won't work,' he abruptly said. 'They would look out of place on the shelf. They won't look like they belong to one family. They will hurt the eye.'

In the corner of my mind, I knew that creating original designs in the USA would be expensive. Rather than debate, I took a chance. I told them: 'We have a limited budget that we can dedicate to original design. I need seven options – two walking style, one for gym-goers and four multi-sports. Can ... you ... guys ... design ... them ... all ... originals?'

Miro and Jeremy stiffened. Once they had relaxed, they agreed with some negotiation ... with a corollary that if the brand succeeded and we went back to them for the second season they would be entitled to an upward fee revision. It sounded reasonable; I agreed.

Exposed

When the first set of designs came in, it was not as much of our appraising Miro and Jeremy's work; it proved to be Miro appraising how much we knew about the subject to be able to appreciate what they had done. For instance, when the designs were presented, we were more concerned with how the sketches 'looked'; Miro was surprised; we must have been his first clients to not ask him about any technical aspect.

These were the first prototype of the sketches.

Over Skype, our ignorance was to be exposed. He asked, 'What are you doing about your "last"?' which I later realized is a technology conversation opener. We hurriedly answered, 'Yes, yes, we have it under control.' There was a question around what kind of rubber should be used; *What do you mean what kind?* was my internal response. As it turned out, there were several rubber varieties that could be employed for the outsole, and Miro needed to know which one we had in mind. We mumbled something about our Chinese manufacturers addressing this. He mentioned the 'heel-to-toe drop' as something that all good performance running shoes possessed; we had not given it a thought. He spoke about material composition (polyurethane or EVA foam) for the midsole. He spoke about the construction of the shoes including strobel, shoe tongue, laces and so on. Greek.

Miro would keep coming back to the 'last'. He would keep reminding us that this was probably the most critical part as it would influence the 'fit'. Besides, his technical specs required the 'last' dimension for him to design the tech-pack.

After a couple of conversations, we confessed. We had no idea. We told him that. Miro blew his top.

When we went to meet Miroslav and Jeremy in Portland to ask him to create original designs for our sports shoe, all we knew was that we wanted an original and attractive design.

We knew we could react to the 'looks' of the shoes. We knew we could guide them on what colours would sell in India. We knew looking at the designs that we would be able to suggest changes.

However, our technical understanding was completely naïve. We thought that Miro and Jeremy would design something on their computer. We would make changes aesthetically without having to worry about last, midsole, outsole, strobel, components, laces, tongue, etc. Once approved aesthetically, we would get the designs on a file. We would give these to our Chinese manufacturer who would convert them into a prototype. We would make changes till a final prototype emerged. We would approve. China would scale the production. We would pay. China would dispatch the shoes to India. We would sell.

Simple.

Miroslav didn't laugh when he got this drift. He used the two words that Sanjeev Agrawal had used when I had told him of my plan to develop India's first home-grown sports brand: *'Think, guys!'*

I prodded him the next day. He said: 'You are in a hurry. You don't have technical knowledge on the development cycle for original designs. Development is the important link between design and production.'

He drew this on his pad to explain.

'Your thinking:

Design --→ Manufacturing

Reality:

Design------------------→ Development----------------------------
----
-- → Manufacturing

'When the Chinese get an idea of how little you know, they will take shortcuts. That will force you to compromise on the design originality. You won't be happy. You will blame the Chinese for the end look. The Chinese will blame us. We will blame everyone else. The ending will not be happy for anyone,' said Miroslav.

'So, what do we do?' we asked. Miroslav suggested: 'Spend more time in China in product development. Carefully select the Chinese factory you seek to work with. Appraise them based on the quality of questions they ask. That will provide you with a hint of their seriousness to produce a great shoe. If you find there are questions you cannot answer, just call me. I will speak on your behalf. And yes, go there and build a prototype. You guys will learn a lot.'

We took that advice. We flew to China.

China, Again, and Again

In July 2017, I returned to China with Rajiv Mehta (who had by now joined the company as a 40 per cent partner) and Samir Saraiya (who was now effectively our man who did everything). We met six factories (tier-2 manufacturing facilities). The Chinese were unfailingly accommodating until you came to the point when you told them that you didn't want anything off-the-shelf but that you would give them the designs and they would have to make from a tech-pack. The Chinese had been happy copying design; they had no proprietary technology. But credit to them, they never refused a challenge. The result: when we sat in their conference rooms to discuss original designs, they would have the materials in-charge, design head, prototype and sample team, midsole expert, outsole professional, the last guys and the owner of the company all in attendance taking notes.

We felt this was going to be simple. However, China presented another challenge. The moment we said we wanted original upper, original midsole and original outsole; they spoke of incremental investments in 'moulds'. A wooden mould for prototype. A steel mould for manufacturing. Moulds for the outsole. Moulds for the midsole. Moulds for components. Their team had a range of questions. We didn't have answers to most.

That is when we began to squirm. Miroslav had provided us a design. Couldn't these Chinese manufacturers simply provide us with a prototype? Why were they making this seemingly simple exercise so complex?

Technology Is Important

That engagement triggered another recall. In the previous months when I would ask the store manager at the Mumbai Adidas store why one shoe would be priced Rs 16,000 and another shoe placed a few feet away exactly half, he would point to the 'midsole' and the next word he would use would be 'technology'.

Midsole. Engine of the running shoe. This is where magic happens. This is where global sports brands invest millions. This then translates into the 'marketing' differentiator. Depending on use, midsole can be a cushion or springy or a mix of both. (It depends on the feel one wants while running or playing. If you don't want to 'feel' the road, you choose cushion; if you want help from your shoe, you choose springy.)

Then come different material densities. Then differentiation. Global chemical majors like BASF, Germany, invest millions in material research on these differentiators in partnership with global footwear majors that we hear as marketing stories. Nike Air comprised technology using air in the midsole; Asics Gel went for technology through the infusion of proprietary gel; Adidas Boost invested in a derivative of the EVA foam with air bubbles to make the shoe pillow-soft, Brooks DNA AMP selected EVA foam with springiness that provided a push to the runner.

The result was that the intensity of technology increased the price of a shoe that made it possible to pay celebrity endorsers, market to millions, post a handsome surplus and keep companies in perpetual motion.

That got us thinking. If we were not investing in contemporary technology were we not compromising the shoe? Were we paying disproportionate attention to the design while overlooking the mechanics? Were we shorting the shoe by taking a midsole designed for another shoe in China and using it on ours? Would a midsole picked off-the-shelf take something away from our marketing spiel when we stood to explain the soul of India's first home-grown running shoe? If the engine of the shoe were commodity, how 'original' could original be?

Second Sustainable Competitive Advantage: Midsole Technology

The brainstorming paid off. We realized we could kill two birds with one stone. A differentiated design for the midsole and investment in moulds would enhance its look. Besides, we could then dictate the material and densities since the moulds were ours. We could play this up in our marketing as well. This would become our second sustainable competitive advantage (we would ramp up the technology quotient in our ads). We opted for original midsole design with contemporary technology … even if that deferred the launch. What were a few months in the grander scheme of doing something that would be remembered for posterity? We would permit nothing to come in the way of our hunger to succeed.

That word 'hunger' triggered a memory. Sunil Bharti Mittal collaborated with Changi Airport to bid for the Mumbai and Delhi airports – and lost both. At an investor conference I attended he was asked why. He said: 'If I had been the same Sunil Mittal selling electronic products before I bid for the telecom license, I would have won both contracts. I was perhaps not as hungry for airports as I had been for the telecom license.'

He later shared the same in an article in *India Today* in 2021 (Punj, 2021).

This then was what it was coming down to. The hunger to produce something India would be proud of: original from design to delivery.

Later, we realized that superior material technology was critical. We met BASF India (subsidiary of BASF Germany, a leader in footwear material technology) and worked with them on several fronts to introduce into India original technology in our third season. Miro also connected us with Algix, a company based in Mississippi that had spent nine years developing Bloom. In 2016, Bloom, an Algix brand, launched the world's first algae-blended EVA as a sustainable ingredient in flexible foams for high-rebound applications such as shoes, sporting products and accessories. We signed an exclusivity contract with Bloom to make eco-conscious footwear in our third season. Trials using Bloom as midsole technology were conducted by our manufacturers in China.

We were still preparing for Season One.

We travelled to China virtually every fortnight thereafter. Partly to learn more about the process. Partly to engage with our manufacturing partners. Partly to stay on their map. Partly to prod them along.

The one thing that began to get on our nerves was the development complexity.

We had heard of technical specifications being fed into a computer and a 3D printer delivering a prototype in a few hours.

Here it was different. The first time we went to China, well after the orders for prototype had been given, the midsole and outsole were not ready. What appeared to be a complex craftsmanship measured in micro-millimetres appeared to us to be needless fine-tuning about something that the consumer would not even appreciate.

Third Sustainable Competitive Advantage: Indian Fit for Indian Feet

When it came to the prototype, the Chinese manufacturer also asked: 'Which "last" do you like?' Their technical team presented a few samples.

Like? Were we supposed to *like* a last? How would one like? How would we even appraise? And that's when we learnt about the last. In sports shoes especially, they say, the 'last' comes first. Last gives the shoe its shape and fit.

At our Hotel Marco Polo in Jinjiang, something interesting transpired. At dinner, Rajiv walked in wearing his G-Star RAW denim. I asked him the reason. 'Fit perfect *chhey*' (it fits perfectly), he replied. In denim, fit is everything, he said. This was our lightbulb moment. I remembered the samples we had ordered for other brands from Myntra and Amazon where my complaint was that they didn't quite fit well. As runners, we had overheard stories about how a particular running shoe brand fit better than the others and the answer inevitably came down to the 'last'. Rajiv and I loved running in Brooks. Though we had never been able to articulate why, that night we encountered our eureka moment – the 'fit' of the Brooks shoe.

I told Rajiv, 'Let us make our "fit" not just most comfortable, but also the most Indian.' Most Indians grew up wearing open footwear because of which their feet widened. The next morning, we had arrived at our third sustainable competitive advantage: an Indian fit. We handed over to the factory in China the Brooks running shoe we had carried and told them make a last that provided us a fit like that. We added that we wanted them to make only two changes: a broader front and a snug heel.

Gradually, a new sense began to creep into our consciousness. Day after day was spent in a factory meeting executives, exploring the complex and struggling to answer questions. We were entrepreneurs; we had explored an unprecedented market opportunity; we knew (or thought we knew) what would sell and at what price.

Truly Indian: our sustainable competitive advantages

What we did not know were the development complexities due to original designs. We did not know measurements. We did not know the science. We could not comprehend the speed.

It took our appointed Chinese manufacturer more than a month just to create the first prototype. A bloody month.

We went through eight rounds of prototyping. From the approved prototype to the maiden delivery took more than seven months. The usual shoe development cycle of 24–30 months (by global brands like Nike with huge R&D teams) we sought to shrink to six. I remember the exasperation: '*Arre joota hi toh hai* (they are just shoes). If they keep delaying like this how will we ever do business?'

This discomfort became more apparent when we flew Miroslav into China to be our intermediary in parrying with Chinese manufacturers for technical queries. Each time we encountered a technical impasse, Miroslav would pass the buck to us. 'You approve the changes to the design; it is your call. It will compromise the look. But it is your call.'

This was the last straw. I was increasingly convinced that this must indeed be the frustration of the usual visionary obstructed by red-tape-worshipping pen-pushers.

So one day in a fit of resentment, I seethed about Miroslav (who had mastered the construction of a shoe from the outside into its inner recess): 'Designer! What does he know of this business anyway?'

As a consolation, we froze the launch date for March 2018 and set about working in line with the stated target.

13

Product Expansion

Thodi aur jaan

We returned from China with samples of sports shoes. I gave them to my running friends to test.

'Try these,' I said expansively.

Beginners who ran 5 km were willing to experiment; long-distancers (marathon runners), who discussed shoes, technology, heel-to-toe drop, weight and cushioning, confessed they wouldn't experiment with the unknown before events. This was a bummer. I was counting them as my customer set.

I realized that to be truly successful, we needed to address the gamut: while our company would cater largely to the beginners (the ones who needed to be jolted out of slumber so to speak), we needed a performance category shoe to address serious runners. Through this approach, we would play the volume game at the middle end and the value game at the premium end (through an outsourced global brand). My conversation with the runner community also provided enough anecdotal evidence on the need for a serious running brand in India. Runners wanted an option to Asics (a leader in running shoes in India then). We sensed an opportunity.

Why not get a global brand hitherto not present in India? The advantages were several. We would attract dedicated runners. The brand would be a serious leadership contender. The pricing would be premium and hence, even with lower volumes we would be able to generate higher revenues and margins. Premium running shoes are priced on an average at Rs 10,000. Even if we sold 50,000 pairs in five years and reported a gross profit of Rs 2,000 per pair, this would enhance our surplus by Rs 10 crore. At 20x gross surplus it could potentially add Rs 200 crore to our valuation across five years.

We decided to go for it.

Fortunately, Rajiv and I were long-distance runners who knew of serious running shoe brands not being retailed in India.

Hoka One One was the brand that ultra-marathoners swore by for the world's thickest midsole at a time when others were thinning them (maximalization versus minimalization). Hoka One One may have been growing globally but it was yet to come to India.

ON was a Swedish brand (in which Roger Federer invested and is a brand ambassador for). It had an attracting midsole with advanced technology and aesthetics. The product was massively popular in Europe and growing in the US, which could have been launched in India.

Brooks was the most popular performance running shoe in the US. The company had been in business for more than 100 years, focused only on performance running shoes. It was a Berkshire Hathaway company (owned by the legendary investor Warren

Buffett), was priced at par with competing brands or lower, and generally figured on the buy list of eight of ten serious runners. Brooks made running shoes, nothing else.

When we engaged with these companies with the standard pitch of how marathons in India had increased from 250 to more than 1,000 a year in the space of just a few years, they surprised us. We felt we had a compelling case – the second most populous giant beginning to awaken and the need for a serious running shoe to compete with Asics. Though they liked the India story, the one thing that they were apprehensive about was the price sensitivity. The result: they conceded that India was on their map, but it would be some years before they would seek to enter the country.

There was one strand of hope. Brooks indicated that if we were ever passing by Seattle, it would be nice if we dropped in for a chat. So, every time we would go to Portland to meet Miro and Jeremy, we would drive three hours to Seattle and meet Brooks.

After a few meetings we struck lucky. Brooks' new Head of International Operations – Justin-Dempsey Chiam – understood Asia. He had lived in Bangladesh; he recognized the untapped India opportunity. The advantage: we didn't need to 'sell' India to him. We did the next best thing: we marketed our vision for Brooks in India. We told them about how running was mainstreaming. We showed him pictures of marathons. I opened www.indiarunning.com on my laptop and showcased that India had over 1,000 runs in 80+ cities. We discussed how Asics, which experimented in India in 2010, was now selling over 3,00,000 pairs. We impressed that Brooks was a better brand. We also shared how two other brands (Mizuno and Saucony) had spoilt their India chances by appointing the wrong distributors. By the end of the conversation, the traction had moved to a different level. 'Can you stay back for a day?' Justin asked, one of the most uplifting things we had heard in a long time.

The following day was a revelation. Brooks indicated that it was keen to explore. We had succeeded in transforming a decisive 'no' into a probable affirmative. We convinced Justin to come to India (which he did during the 2018 Tata Mumbai Marathon). We introduced him to runners and running groups; we visited the markets of Mumbai, Bengaluru and Delhi. On his last day before he left for Seattle, he said, 'Let's do this!'

This is what the Brooks distribution agreement meant: enhanced credibility (considering that in the performance running category Brooks was ahead of Nike, Saucony, Adidas, Asics and Hoka One One in the US), respect (being the first Warren Buffett subsidiary to enter India) and seamless technology thought-leadership (in late 2017, it was designing shoes they would market in 2022; one of its technologists had worked on the Usain Bolt running shoe in which he created a 100 metre world record).

Besides Brooks' running shoes, we agreed to buy lifestyle shoes to create a premium Heritage collection; we agreed to buy an inventory of its Warren Buffett collection backed with the image of Warren Buffett inside our stores; we signed to create two exclusive Brooks retail stores with all its merchandise.

We had, in the course of our journey, started entertaining the idea that we weren't just building a sports brand; we were creating a platform.

We would be providing space to complementary brands that would strengthen the sales platform. What this meant was that we would be open to merchandizing other global and Indian brands that would strengthen our consumer pull, attract larger footfalls and put us in a position where we could cross-sell other products.

And it just so happened that while we were grappling with the Brooks (shoes and apparel) dilemma, revenues, supply chain and cash flows, a third product popped up on the horizon.

Caps.

One of Rajiv's friends dropped the word that New Era caps was looking for an India partner. New Era was the most respected the world over when it came to caps or headgear. New Era wasn't a brand; it was an icon. Exclusive partners of the NBA, NFL, MLB, Man U, Spurs, Disney and Marvel. More relevant to us, New Era had entered into an exclusive partnership with Virat Kohli in India. Besides, every other day some Hindi film star – Ranbir Kapoor, Ranveer Singh, Anil Kapoor, Farhan Akhtar, Sonakshi Sinha, Alia Bhatt and so on – would be posing in a New Era cap.

Brooks was top of the line; now New Era was coming into our fold. We could have been excused into believing that our platform was working.

We engaged with New Era. We told them how we would want to build New Era for the retail market in India. We possessed a proprietary footprint of seventeen stores. We enjoyed a growing online presence. We would build a New Era e-commerce store. We would get New Era into Future Group outlets, Shoppers Stop and Lifestyle. We would get an Indian IPL team to adopt New Era headgear.

New Era heard us with wide-eyed interest. What the company insisted on was that we invest in customized store fixtures since there was a specific way it required New Era caps to be showcased and marketed. We pursued New Era with the vigour of a besotted who has stolen his first glance of someone stunning who has just walked into the room.

D:FY became the exclusive India partner to New Era, the world's iconic cap company. There was better news in store: to offset the cash flow squeeze on account of our investment into fixtures as recommended by New Era, the company agreed to provide us credit.

More positives emerged after we had put out the official press release. There was a call from Mumbai Indians; it sounded keen to get into an arrangement. In seven days, we were the official fan cap makers for Mumbai Indians (India's most successful IPL cricket team). Thereafter we received a call from the team of Rohit Sharma, Indian cricket team's vice-captain; he was keen to explore an 'RS' signature line in exchange for a revenue-sharing deal.

The word got back to New Era. In just two months, we had surprised its leadership team sitting in London of the vast possibilities within India.

We started telling ourselves that this was the start of a journey that had commenced with our brand all right but was now taking us into exciting uncharted terrains.

As an early investor in cleartrip.com and a keen follower of the space, one thing was emerging from consumer-tech businesses. The 'platform' was not just a preferred investible standalone brand but more valuable. For instance, Amazon.in, flipkart.com, tatacliq.com, ajio.com, nykaa.com and purple.com are platforms where you sell multiple brands. Standalone brand stores are online stores where you get just that brand.

We had earned the respect of two successful global brands. We were now prospecting wider possibilities.

14

The Brand Story

Vande Mataram

After I returned from China in May 2017, there was a priority in freezing the brand name and logo.

These were critical, as in the sports gear business, the logo becomes more prominent than the brand name, featuring as a design element on merchandized shoes and apparel. This is what one needed as well: the logo of our company needed to become a hook by which it would be recalled.

I engaged with a strategic brand management firm with a reputation for understanding Indianness. After a few engagements I gave up: it may have understood India by the virtue of living in India, but it could not grasp the utility of a sports logo as a design differentiator and an identity in itself (like the Nike Swoosh and Adidas three stripes).

When I began to look international, I came across Tomek in London. For £3,000 he presented us options on the name of our company and logo. During a conversation with Vinod Naidu (Sachin Tendulkar's former business manager) on a leisurely walk through Indiranagar in Bengaluru, we discovered that his brother managed a creative agency. During a brainstorming session, I dropped a question: 'On the walk we just took, which hoarding stood out?' Each one thought for a while and then mentioned. Interestingly, the brand that each one mentioned (WROGN) had captured the attention more for the name than for the celebrity in it (Virat Kohli).

We wanted the agency to build on the core idea of what we needed to communicate: that we were a brand that defied convention; that we were a brand that was taking established concepts head-on; that this was going to be a sports shoe with an attitude. The word that began to play on every one's palate was 'defy'. We were here to defy. We were here to disrupt. The result is that after some wordsmithing, we arrived at how the name would look. The verb became the noun. We dropped the 'E' and added ':'. This is what we finalized: D:FY.

Now came the logo. Tomek presented interesting options. My filters: the logo required dynamism, athletic spirit, and a flexibility to be used at any angle on any product (shoe or apparel). Finally, we got a logo that drew inspiration from 'lightning', was 'sporty' enough, possessed the sharpness of the swoosh and the expanse of the three stripes. This is how it looked:

The D:FY logo would be colour-neutral. It could be blue, black, red, orange, violet or teal … whatever the designer wanted. However, when used as a corporate logo, we settled for blue and orange in line with the colours of the Indian cricket team.

We had capital. We had a business. We had a product. We had an identity.

The last addition – getting to the name and the logo – had set us back Rs 10 lakh.

A business is built around dreams.

Hardik Pandya, Here to Defy

My dream was an Indian cricket team with the D:FY logo on their chests while the national anthem played in the background. Another was our perspiring sports ambassador looking down from a giant hoarding at thousands of runners snaking past Haji Ali, Mumbai, during the Tata Mumbai Marathon. The third was figuring on the cover of business magazines explaining the D:FY success story. The fourth was ringing the bell on the Bombay Stock Exchange.

D:FY needed a popular sportsman to be memorable. A cricketer ideally.

There was a fetish when it came to cricket. Until I moved to Mumbai, I had not missed an international cricket match at Eden Gardens. I was there for all the venue's big moments: when Sunil Gavaskar was dismissed for a duck facing Malcom Marshall in the 1983 Test series. When Sachin bowled the final over against South Africa in the Hero Cup. When Azharuddin scored a century on his Test debut. When England and Australia played the Reliance World Cup final. When V.V.S. Laxman and Rahul Dravid created an epic partnership that powered India to victory after following on. When the crowd sprinkled bottles on the ground when Sachin was run out against Pakistan. When India lost to Sri Lanka in the 1996 World Cup semi-final. Or even when I gave away Man of the Match awards when Future Group sponsored a Test series in England and Ireland.

We could not afford Virat Kohli, M.S. Dhoni or Rohit Sharma as brand ambassadors; we needed someone who embodied the spirit of defiance but would still be affordable. Anil Kumble recommended Hardik Pandya, who bowled consistently at 140+ kmph at nets and hit the longest sixes in the modern game. Kumble went one step ahead: if India were to win abroad, there was no way it could do so without Hardik. The word he used with 'place' was 'permanent'. He predicted that Hardik, like Kohli, Dhoni and Sharma, would play all forms of the game for the country (Tests, ODIs and T20s).

Hardik played for Mumbai Indians and was represented by IMG Reliance. Vinod Naidu, now a D:FY shareholder, knew them well. Besides, Vinod had represented Tendulkar for nineteen years, which positioned us better for the attention of IMG Reliance. We explained our plans to IMG Reliance. We were told we were a challenger brand and would be a gear fit for Hardik as he had captured the brand's attitude. Vinod played this to our advantage; he argued that Hardik would be overpowered by the bigger ambassador of this brand while at D:FY he would be the only one. We would provide Hardik visibility on hoardings and inside our stores, who could then take the high road of having partnered a truly Indian sports brand.

Thereafter, it was time to pitch to Hardik. At Chennai, where we met him, Hardik entered the room wearing black tracks, a loose t-shirt and a thick gold chain with the HP logo. He didn't just walk into the room; he strode. He wasn't just Hardik

Pandya at that moment; it could have been a gum-chewing Vivian Richards.

I turned to an old ally to break the ice. '*Kem chhey* (How are you?), Hardik,' I said. His eyes lit up. A connect had been established. For the next hour, one engaged shamelessly in the vernacular, drawing references to Vadodara (in Gujarat, India, where he lived). Thereafter, Rajiv took over in Gujarati to explain his Puma days. Then back to me to explain the big picture we saw and what we wanted to build.

Hardik wanted to examine the product he was to endorse. We didn't have any. We showed him Miro's designs instead; he loved them.

When Rajiv began to explain the technology of what was then under development, Hardik asked if we could design customized cricket shoes. As the conversation progressed, it became increasingly apparent that Hardik had no interest in being a passive brand ambassador. He desired to engage; he was keen to contribute to product design from the perspective of a user; he was keen to wear our shoes out on the field; he explained how when he needed to change his shoes on the ground, he could draw the attention of the TV cameras to the D:FY shoe. He spoke to us about how he could push the product to his growing social media following. During the course of the engagement, something interesting had begun to happen: when the conversation had begun he would use phrases like '*Tamaare aa karvu joiyye*' (you should do this); by the close the conversation had moved to '*Aapre aa karshu*' (we will do this). From 'you' he had started using 'we'; from 'should do' he had started using 'we will'. He sealed his consent with 'Done! *Hoon tamaari saathe chhu*' (I am with you).

We had found our ambassador.

Jolt Out of Slumber

Remember the time when I had felt that Santosh Desai and his team had read our prospects wrong?

Well, we went back to him.

He would now get a picture of how we were different and position our brand the way it deserved.

Future Brands, Santosh's company, came up with an interesting proposition. It emphasized that Indians were cerebral; in India, mind prevailed over the body; the country dedicated itself to the intellectual over the physical. To prove this, Santosh said that India produces one of the largest number of engineering graduates but one of the lowest number of Olympic medal winners.

What's that got to do with our brand? we asked.

Simple, he said. As India has become increasingly global, the mindset of the mind over body is beginning to change. Sport is becoming mainstream. It is becoming fancy to get fit or *even seen to be wanting to get fit.* The result is that sports gear – sports shoes and the dry-fit T-shirts – is becoming essential to the wardrobe. There are far more wannabe fitness consumers than those that are actually serious about it. The pronouncement: D:FY should target the 95 per cent who *want* to be fit over the 5 per cent who *are* fit.

Santosh added that while this was the big idea, this would need to be communicated with the corresponding emotion that inspired people to go out, buy D:FY, step out of lethargy, run, walk and exercise. His words: 'Let D:FY *jolt you out of slumber.*'

If we positioned D:FY around this act of defiance against lethargy and convention, then the brand would be relevant to the country's large sedentary population. Besides, it would create a unique identity distinct from that of the heavyweights (Nike, Adidas, etc.) who targeted only the serious.

The firepower of our brand spending, the image of Hardik Pandya and the sophistication that we brought into our communication would now generate the desired impact: not merely communicate with the prospect ... but jolt him/her.

We believed that the power of our messaging – 'D:FY EVERYDAY' – would connect with someone with a wheat or beer belly, inspiring the person to try our product, wear it, jog, play sport and become fitter. Besides, if this was the first time that someone was stretching out in years, then one did not need to do that in a Nike or an Adidas. D:FY would be the best point to begin – Indian in origin, Indian in price.

We were not merely marketing a product; we were building an emotion.

15

Bollywood Connect

Dil Chahta Hai

Hardik Pandya, brand ambassador. Anil Kumble, mentor. The unknown D:FY was gaining currency.

The priority was to build a brand that would enhance corporate longevity, recall and valuation.

In the preceding years, one had seen how challenging brands (offline and online) were getting differential valuations. There were successful instances like Dream11, Byju's, Nykaa, Paper Boat, Bira, Raw Pressary, Wrogn, HRX and Vahdam that had challenged existing brands to build markets and enhance value.

Besides, cricket and Hindi film celebrities were partnering brands beyond ambassadorial capacity. Hrithik collaborated with HRX, Tiger Shroff with Prowl, Sonam Kapoor with Rheason, Deepika Padukone with All About You, Anushka Sharma with Nush, Wrogn and One 8 with Virat Kohli, and Seven with M.S. Dhoni.

We recognized that the Bollywood angle was missing in our story. Through our network, we approached agencies that managed Akshay Kumar and Aamir Khan. Their coming in as equity investors and brand ambassadors would help us position D:FY distinctively and help us build a wider distribution (mom and pop) network. We never heard back from them.

But something interesting transpired instead.

I am a compelling Web series geek on OTT platforms. One such Emmy-nominated series was *Inside Edge*, made by Excel Entertainment. The storyline was woven around the popular Indian Premier League (IPL) cricket tournament. What was interesting was that on the one hand it was on serious cricket (IPL-line tournament) and on the other there was a drama that extended beyond the cricket. It was racy, pacy and cutting-edge. The actors and direction were compelling. The producers ensured every episode positioned cricket in the lead. I sensed an opportunity. We could piggyback *Inside Edge* to enter the world of films and Web series entertainment.

We reached out to *Inside Edge*'s makers to explore a partnership as its merchandise-cum-marketing partner for Season 2. We pitched to the content makers – Excel Entertainment – to consider us as its sports gear partner (where every team would wear the D:FY logo on their jersey similar to Nike on the Indian cricket team). Besides, *Inside Edge* was showcased on Amazon Prime, and Amazon was our potential exclusive online partner, making even more sense. Besides, when I researched the promotion for *Inside Edge* Season One, Amazon Prime had splurged. There were hoardings all over Mumbai at prime locations. The hoarding showcased players (actors) in their cricket gear. I could visualize the D:FY logo displayed prominently. Best of all, *Inside Edge* was the only Indian Web series to be nominated for an Emmy (Scroll, 2018).

We reached out. We got an appointment with Vishal Ramchandani, the company's marketing head.

Excel Entertainment is owned by Farhan Akhtar and Ritesh Sidhwani (with a track record of having produced films like *Dil Chahta Hai*, *Don*, *Don 2*, *Rock On*, *Zindagi Na Milegi Dobara*, *Dil Dhadakne Do*, *Fukrey*, *Raees*, *Gold* and *Gully Boy*). They liked our idea. It turned out that their marketing head Vishal was a sneaker freak; when we showcased our products, he asked, 'What *else* can we do together?'

A few days later, Vishal asked us to pitch directly to Ritesh Sidhwani, co-founder of Excel Entertainment and among the most successful film producers in India. Ritesh was wearing Cargo trousers and a Henley tee. In a minute, he put us at ease. My investor relations and stock-picking experiences proved handy; Rajiv's background, as someone who had built Puma India from scratch, provided comfort. We told him how big we thought the business could become: 450 stores in ten years; Rs 2,000 crore revenues by then. What turned him on was that we had invested our life's savings in the venture. We had 'skin in the game'.

Then he asked to see our products. He tried every shoe. Checked how it looked in the mirror. Asked us the price. No reaction on his face. Then he asked: 'How can I help?'

We told him that getting to showcase our products in his next film could expand our market. Given that we were a start-up, we could scarcely afford the usual product placement fee, so we would have to think of some other structure. He asked what kind. I told him that we were not raising money at that time, but we could make an exception and give them a stake in our company at par in return for product placement. He liked what he heard. Before getting into specifics, he added, 'Let me get you time with Farhan.'

Farhan Akhtar was going to be an interesting pitch. Farhan had started his career as a director; his first film *Dil Chahta Hai* was cult-cracking. Thereafter, Farhan transformed into an accomplished actor, one of his memorable performances being *Bhaag Milkha Bhaag*. There was no air around Farhan when we met him, dressed in casual denim shorts and a tee. It was a fan boy moment. Being into fitness, I was in awe to see him. I had loved his singing in *Rock On*. Besides, as an entrepreneur, I had appreciated Excel's differentiated business model that emphasized youth-directed content.

I showcased our effort. There was a pause and softness in my voice. I paused to communicate that I was a big fan and appreciated what he had accomplished.

He 'listened' patiently without interruption. He thanked me for the appreciation. He congratulated us on our vision. In turn, he explained how, while he was training for *Bhaag Milkha Bhaag*, his 100 metre best was just a few seconds slower that the Indian record of 10.26 seconds. He appreciated our commitment to create a truly Indian and affordable sports brand, an important starting point for any athlete.

Then it was time to show Farhan our products. This was routine. Every meeting we went to we carried two suitcases filled with shoes and apparel samples. By now, we could open the suitcase, line our products in a planned sequence: walking shoes, multi-sport shoes and gym shoes. As we showcased, I would explain the fine print of each product, including the midsole, upper material and construction.

Farhan saw them, tried a few, embarrassingly requested us to pack and apologized for our having taken the trouble to meet him. I wanted to ask for his autograph, but on second thoughts, felt embarrassed.

The following day, Ritesh called to discuss the partnership. Even as he was fine with the equity stake, there was a gap in what we wanted to offer and what he sought. I did not seek to negotiate (drawing from my experience with Kishore Biyani that if the gap is not too large, it is better to give first and request for a take later). I agreed. I requested that Farhan should become our ambassador and not endorse any other sports brand. Ritesh agreed.

Now we had Hardik Pandya, Farhan Akhtar and Anil Kumble on our page. For a company of our size with no revenues and marketing only still a dream, this was a win. Make it 'big win'.

16

High Risk, High Return Bet

Mila mauka, maaro chauka

Bold is beautiful.

The product and brand strategies were in place.
We now needed to freeze the D:FY retail experience.

We needed to be in the right malls; we needed to be in the right zone of that mall; we needed to build a world-class retail experience.

The rationale was that the shoes would be tested over time, but the stores would be appraised immediately.

We were optimistic that if we created a store that would seduce a passer-by into walking in, half the battle would be won. For this to happen, the D:FY store would need to look different. We evaluated designers; we eventually went with a global retail experience design agency called I-AM. The brief: we needed to look different from Nike, Adidas, Puma and Reebok; we needed the store to be designed at a moderate cost.

I-AM delivered a premium retail experience. The look was described as 'masculine' where raw elements (cement blocks, thick wires, orange steel rods, grey walls, rough ground, racetrack and open lighting) were exposed. This was not minimalistic; this was raw and stark in line with our 'defy' positioning; in the store we would celebrate cricket, football, badminton, tennis and other sports.

The design also created a separate runner's zone, where we showcased Brooks running shoes including the Heritage and Warren Buffett collection. We introduced for the first time in India a unique proprietary technology by Brooks called Run Signature. It was high-tech. We offered every customer the Run Signature technology to select a customized shoe by doing a sensor-led GAIT analysis that extended beyond just the foot to the knee and spine. Brooks Run Signature was more advanced and focused on the entire kinetic chain – foot strike, knee impact and hips. We imported sensors from the US. Run Signature required a treadmill and specific lighting. Every D:FY store offered this for free. It made our store not just look good but also serious about performance running. More importantly, it changed a runner's mindset from buying a good-looking shoe to buying a shoe that would minimize injuries.

The store also comprised a separate fixture for New Era caps with premium-ness and positioning that could transport one to any New Era global store.

Unlike our competition, where the store experience was defined by global teams and had gone minimalistic, we preferred not to whisper. As you walked by the store, you had a larger-than-life image of Hardik Pandya welcoming you into the store. Inside, we had Anil Kumble's images that spoke on technology differentiators. There was the Brooks imagery with treadmill and images of Warren Buffett. And then the New Era fixture with different caps like NY, Boston Celtics, Chicago Bulls and Virat Kohli. The lighting was yellow and the music sporty. We had racetrack lines running through the stores and on to the walls. The trial rooms looked like locker rooms of prominent global sports teams. We invested in unique slanting mirrors below the shoe display so that anyone who tried the shoe did not have to walk to where the mirrors were.

Most people we showed this to privately said *'Aisa toh kabhi kisi sports store mein dekha nahi'* (Haven't seen anything like this is a sports store before).

We had arrived at base camp.

Aggression, and How

Initially we found it difficult to get retail space in malls.

As Mumbai's retail infrastructure consolidated, the players reduced to a few prominent brands like Phoenix Mills, Blackstone, Rahejas, Infinity, Prestige and Forum. With the decline in choice, it was becoming increasingly difficult for a new brand to rent prime retail space. Rajiv and I sweated our network; Amit Dabriwala, my ex-boss at United Credit, helped. Amit had moved to Mumbai and was a Board Member at Phoenix Mills. I shared our D:FY story with Amit, who was proud to see an ex-employee attempting to defy the odds. Amit promised to advocate my case with the head of the space leasing business at Phoenix Mills.

I was also known to the Phoenix Mills Managing Director Atul Ruia through my Future Group background (High Street Phoenix, India's biggest mall success story, had been indebted to Big Bazaar and Pantaloons footfalls). When I started my investor relations firm in 2009, Phoenix Mills was my client. There were enough references. Besides, Rajiv as the former Puma MD also knew senior retail infrastructure executives. Amit's reference proved decisive: Phoenix yielded space in three malls (Kurla in Mumbai, Palladium in Chennai and Phoenix United Mall in Bareilly, Lucknow).

The search for the right mall took months before we zeroed in on Phoenix Marketcity in Kurla, Mumbai. The next sixteen mall spaces we signed in just forty-five days.

Because we had faced 'Sorry, no space to spare' on so many occasions, the relief at being able to get any space turned to gluttony: we signed spaces from 500 square feet to 3,500 square feet; we signed twenty malls in eight cities; we agreed to expensive rents convincing ourselves that given the relatively small spaces in some cases, the total outgo would be on the lower side and our lower overheads would make it possible for us to recover the incremental rent quicker. When the space was larger, we justified our contract on the ground that, yes, there would be a correspondingly larger outgo on account of furniture, fixtures, air conditioning and inventory that would translate into higher operating expenditure, rent, common area maintenance, energy, people cost and security deposit, but we would be able to recoup all from a 'wow' experience that would generate higher footfall.

The retail business is about higher footfall. If you enjoy a decent conversion, then you make higher revenues. If your revenues are high, the costs, though high, do not increase proportionately with revenues, which makes higher rents affordable.

We had an argument to counter every challenge. Nothing could possibly come in the way of a plan that we felt would transform the Indian world of sports gear. We preferred high risk, high return always. That was the mindset.

This is how our Rs 10 crore retail capital expenditure was allocated: Rs 6 crore towards store décor and Rs 4 crore allocated towards security deposit equivalent to 7.5 months' rent (which we didn't quite take as 'cost', considering that it would be returned if we ever closed down or moved out).

The twenty stores we planned to get operational in under ninety days was the largest and fastest rollout by any Indian sports retailer building a business from scratch.

17

Online Partnership

Mujhse shaadi karogi

The prototypes for our sports shoes and apparel were ready. Looked good, fit right. We signed ten stores. Our Bengaluru office was up and ready. We signed Hardik Pandya the cricketer. Grey Worldwide and Future Brands were on board. We had an interesting story in the making.

It was time to test the product, brand and story online.

Flipkart, Myntra and Amazon had transformed the way Indians (especially the youth) shopped. They had taken aspirations to small towners. This was an important channel for us – for brand building and sales conversion. After electronics, the fastest growing segment on these platforms was sports. Puma had led this category online. Both Amazon and Myntra (part of Flipkart) knew Rajiv well.

We met the Myntra fashion top brass first (sports was part of the fashion category). We presented our story with passion. The opportunity as we saw (for a mid-market truly Indian sports brand); the China market analogy and ANTA; the trip to Canton Fair; how we had engaged ex-New Balance and Keen designers in Portland to create original, bold design; my experience with Future Group; the investments in moulds for original midsole and outsole design; the creation of an original 'last' that imparted a unique Indian fit (broad in the front, snug at the heel); bold on colours and number of SKUs; the upper material – flyknit and double-layered engineered mesh; emphasis on creating a brand; the engagements of Anil Kumble, Hardik Pandya and Grey Worldwide; pricing range from Rs 2,000 to Rs 5,000; investing Rs 20 crore of seed capital; the differentiated feel of our stores; our store line-up in Phoenix Mills, Inorbit and VR Malls; the launch event.

We spoke for an hour. Non-stop.

Then we opened our suitcase. We insisted they try our shoes. They could not fault the shoes.

After ninety minutes, they said, 'Can we make this an exclusive Myntra-Flipkart launch?' We said we wanted to work exclusively with either them or Amazon. We desired to know how exclusivity would help us in terms of sales and revenue.

So Myntra gave us their spiel. That they were thought and market leaders when it came to fashion and sports. That in the past twelve months two big brands had chosen to go exclusively with them (over Amazon). They shared their insights on the sports category. They said that on their platform D:FY would generate far more revenues than on Amazon. Their marketing executive told us about the positioning we would get on the Myntra homepage, hoardings and launch. There was a human connect.

When we stepped out, Rajiv and I smiled. I said, 'F*ck Amazon, let's go with Myntra–Flipkart.' The patient Rajiv said, 'Let's hear Amazon first.'

The next day, we went to Amazon. I was in awe of this icon brand (having read *The Everything Store* and the journey of Jeff Bezos). Amazon and Myntra–Flipkart proved culturally different. Amazon came across as more process-led than people-led. Even to enter Amazon offices, you needed to sign a Visitor's Non-Disclosure Agreement. There was no receptionist; there are security guards. Your visitor's badge had a code that was scanned. You called the person with whom you had a meeting. He/she came and ushered you into a meeting room. You fetched your own tea/coffee.

The D:FY-thon commenced. Same pitch. Same passion. Same story. The entire Amazon and Cloudtail (selling partner of Amazon) senior team leading sports category appeared to hear. We opened our suitcase, displayed the sample shoes and apparel.

Same result.

They were completely in awe of our product creation. They tried the shoes. Liked them a lot. We spoke about creating a brand led by offline retail. The discussion came down to the same bottom line: Amazon desired exclusivity too.

They showcased the work Amazon had done to launch New Balance and Under Armour (large global brands as exclusive Amazon partnerships) in India. They spoke about their marketing muscle. They looked at the sports category getting larger and agreed to our positioning at 95 per cent Indians than the premium minority. Rather than telling us what they could do for us as an exclusive partner, they asked, 'What do you want from us?'

'We will be signing ten more stores and have twenty stores to retail from. In the sports category, we recognize the importance of touch-and-feel. I am confident we will own our consumers, so we may not need your help there,' I spoke.

Amazon disagreed. They said, offline and online have their share of exclusive customers. They spoke of their impending partnership with Future Group. Then I said that since we had built this from scratch, we needed two things. We needed Amazon to 'buy' a certain minimum quantity from us, we needed marketing dollars from Amazon, and we needed visibility on Amazon.in.

Amazon did not agree immediately, but they said that if we were to provide it exclusivity, both could be possible.

I told Rajiv privately, 'My vote is for Amazon.'

The next week was hectic. We were shooting with Hardik and Anil Kumble in Mumbai. Both Myntra and Amazon wanted Hardik and Anil Kumble to do videos saying, 'D:FY, available exclusively on Amazon/Myntra.' We used the shoot to get them to commit. Myntra was the first to commit to putting D:FY on several of their hoardings for a week before and after launch. They also told us to expect Myntra/Flipkart/Jabong to sell ~20,000 pairs shoes and ~30,000 apparel in the first six months. They spoke about the launch date coinciding with our launch. But they were clear: they would not buy our product. They would leverage all available data to 'push' D:FY on Flipkart, Myntra and Jabong.

Amazon took time to decide. Amazon needed to get its IMC (marketing) team to commit. It needed Cloudtail to commit on the numbers. It needed the marketing team to commit on visibility for Prime Day on Amazon.in.

We were midday in the shoot. There were only a few hours left. We told Amazon, 'Sorry, but we are going ahead with Myntra.' Their lady (incidentally a Bengali) said, *Tomaar help dorkaar. Aar ek ghonta daao* (Need your help in getting one more hour). You won't regret.' By this time, Myntra's delivery boxes had arrived for Hardik and Anil Kumble to shoot.

At 5.00 p.m., Amazon called. 'We will buy 12,000 pairs of shoes and 15,000 apparel pieces to start with. We will invest up to Rs 2 crore jointly on advertising (25 per cent of the Rs 8 crore we told them we would be spending). We will launch you on Amazon Prime Day. D:FY will feature in our print ad in all newspapers under "Exclusive launch". D:FY will be showcased on all promotions of Amazon. We will give you prime real estate on Amazon.in for a week after Prime Day.'

Amazon was offering real money. It would have skin in the game. We said yes. Hardik and Anil Kumble were photographed with an Amazon delivery box in their hands.

We apologized to Myntra. Its senior leadership promised to not work with D:FY for at least two years.

Next week, we were back at Amazon offices in Bengaluru for the D:FY launch on Amazon's Prime Day on 16 July.

That's when I realized the power of process led by people (and how it came to haunt us). At Amazon, the process wins. Every relevant team member was present. Members from Amazon category, platform marketing, external marketing (IMC) and Cloudtail. Our products were still getting ready in China. We decided to airlift some for the Prime Day Launch. Plus I was looking forward to waking up with the D:FY logo on the *TOI* front page.

Then came the tricky part: margins and discount discussion.

Since we were overconfident, I insisted that D:FY would not be ridiculously discounted on Amazon. Brand before sales, I told them. I was confident that would sell enough offline. Their process was defined. If we wanted a pricing decision, then we needed to offer them 100 per cent stock correction. This meant that if they had unsold quantities, we would be bound to replace all with new products. This meant that unsold inventory could flow back to us (they explained this as stock correction and not return). So confident was I that it didn't bother me much. There was one more advantage. If we chose 100 per cent stock correction, the margin that they would deduct would be lower.

The lady managing the Cloudtail function told us that we needed to be flexible and take it as it came. The online rules were different; they were about fear and greed and discounts played to that. I disagreed. I believed that our product with the story – original design, original Indian fit, original midsole and outsole technology – would inspire consumers to buy at the full price.

The Amazon content team insisted that the online business was all about content. Every product needed a description. We also needed to build a brand store inside Amazon detailing the history of the brand, founders, products, story with images and videos. Online shoppers would 'click' to know about a new brand.

Amazon went into what I now call reality. The AI (artificial intelligence) engine at Amazon is built in a manner that the higher the clicks on D:FY products , the quicker our hierarchy would change when someone searched for sports shoes or apparels. The result was that if more customers clicked on D:FY, the next time they came shopping, they would view D:FY more than anything else. I remembered Kishore Biyani explain this to an analyst. In retail, good money chases good products. What sells gets prime shelf space. This is what Amazon was saying as well.

I was not entirely happy. I had assumed that being an exclusive Amazon partner, I would be privileged. This was not how things were turning out. As an Amazon exclusive partner, we would get confirmed purchase, Prime Day launch and Rs 2 crore. Amazon would obviously push D:FY since it owned inventory and would spend Rs 2 crore. But they warned us: we needed to change our perspective on discounts and volume on their platform. Higher volume was the only key to get higher visibility.

We said we would take it as it came.

This then was the final order from Cloudtail: 12,000 pairs of D:FY shoes, 2,000 pairs of Brooks and 12,000 pieces of apparel and accessories. The total gross merchandise value (GMV) of the first order was Rs 9 crore! I did a back-of-the-envelope calculation. Annualized GMV for the full first year would be at least Rs 20–25 crore. This alone would give us a valuation of Rs 150 crore ... and the retail story was yet to unfold.

18

Skin in the Game

Khud pe yakeen

As we were executing our plans, we began to get requests from venture funds and family offices to induct them as investors.

The moral dilemma: if we were confident of what we were doing and possessed adequate capital, why take from others? If we were not confident and possessed the capital, there was all the more reason not to take capital from others.

I had read the book *Skin in the Game* by Nassim Nicholas Taleb and this is the point he made. He gave examples of how politicians and administrators never had skin in the game and hence were not the best allocators of the taxpayer's money. There was a famous quote by the legendary investor George Soros: 'It does not matter whether you are right or wrong. It matters how much money you made when you are right and how much money you lost when you were wrong.' Taleb also wrote that ideas that are manifested by skin in the game tend to do better because you have *skin in the game* and that you will *do* what is right than what others *think* is right.

I did not consider raising external capital as de-risking. If I was sure of myself and possessed the money, why was I even considering taking other people's cash?

There was also the rewards carrot. I knew that if I assumed all the risk, all the rewards would be mine. This was driven by a confidence in our competence in building a truly Indian sports brand. I could not see how we could fail.

The decision became simple. I would be killing three birds. One: morality; two: my confidence; three: autonomy.

Because we had not mobilized external capital, we enjoyed autonomy. We were our own bosses. Every decision flowed from what was right for the business.

I chose to see the rewards and not the risks.

Here are some decisions we took:

1. Aggressive mindset: Because we believed we cut no corners, never took a shortcut, we chose to bat on the front foot. We knew we had something special. We played aggressively.

2. Our vision was to build a truly Indian sports brand. We hired footwear designers from Portland and apparel designers from Italy. We did not compromise by copying designs of Nike or Adidas.

3. We chose to work with tier-2 factories in China (not tier-3). The quality of the product and the finish was primary. Our products couldn't look inferior to competition. We wanted our customers to get the best value. Since tier-2 factories took minimum order quantity of 1,000 units per

colour, that meant 34,000 pairs of footwear and 1,00,000 pieces of apparel in the first season. The total bill for the first season's inventory worked out to Rs 8 crore.

4. We became exclusive India partners of Brooks and New Era because we believed they were complementary brands that delivered value to customers. We launched two exclusive Brooks stores in India at our cost. We ordered the best Brooks running shoes for Indian runners. We invested in New Era fixtures so that the brand reflected its salience. We partnered with Mumbai Indians and Rohit Sharma for New Era at our cost. Total investment: Rs 4 crore.

5. We opened seventeen stores in seven cities in under three months, our biggest expenditure. No other sports brand (including global) had done this in its opening year. We chose a high cap-ex cum high op-ex model. Total cost: Rs 8 crore. We desired to build an Indian sports brand. We worked with Future Brands on the strategy and philosophy. We worked with Grey Worldwide for our creatives. We hired three digital agencies. We enlisted Hardik Pandya, Anil Kumble, Farhan Akhtar, Jaipur Pink Panthers and *Inside Edge* Season 2 as partners. Our first campaign was launched in the most expensive media month of Diwali. Total cost: Rs 4 crore.

6. Rather than going wide, we went deep with e-commerce. We partnered exclusively with Amazon. At that time, the brand was more important than sales.

7. We hired an international retail design firm to design our stores. When customers walked inside our stores, we wanted them to feel like they had entered a Nike or Adidas store. Even the great Biyani appreciated what his apprentice had achieved.

And this is the point. When you have the skin in the game, the perspective changes. A former colleague started a technology venture almost at the same time. Despite being wealthy, he chose to de-risk and not put his skin in the game. He often seeks me out to be introduced to potential investors. And I keep asking myself, what prevents him from putting his own money? If everything he says is what he will deliver, why share the rewards? Why not put your money where your mouth is? And for this one reason, I found it difficult to recommend him.

I built D:FY with all my skin-in-the-game. There were temptations to divest but morality took precedence. Thanks to the greed (rewards before risks). And ego (we were doing everything right).

19

Devil's Advocate

Soch lo Thakur!

While preparing for the launch, I showcased the business model to someone I trusted.

I presented our approach to Utpal Sheth, my close friend and Rakesh Jhunjhunwala's partner. I went to Utpal with a suitcase of samples. Utpal ushered me into the conference room at RARE where I had done several meetings sitting on the other side and asking prospective investee companies a range of searching questions. This time, I was required to answer.

I laid the collection on the large conference room table, starting with walking, multi-sport and gym shoes. I showcased Brooks and New Era. I displayed the apparel that matched the shoes. Utpal invited his sister Ushma to appraise the merchandise. They wore a number of shoes as I provided a running commentary on attributes and price points.

'Very comfortable,' Ushma said. 'Great job, PD!'

'Brilliant, Prashant, well done,' said Utpal. '*Superb chhey* (they are great). You have certainly come a long way.'

'Tell me how I can help …'

'Punch holes in my business model,' I said.

Utpal had evaluated consumer-facing businesses like Titan, VIP, Future Group, Metro Shoes and others. He understood the business models of such businesses. Utpal enquired about our model and execution plan. I explained how we planned to launch twenty stores in ninety days and enter into an exclusive deal with either Amazon or Myntra. I told him about our marketing plans and brand ambassadors.

Utpal speaks slowly. That day he could have provided excellent shorthand practice. 'Prashant,' he said, 'you are setting up a high cap-ex, high op-ex and high working capital execution plan. This represents a high risk. You need to de-risk the model. In the overall scheme of things, your conviction may be rewarded … but before that your patience will be tested.'

I remember Utpal's last words. 'Why this hurry? Yaar, even Rome was not built in a day.'

Utpal's gist: start small, experiment, make affordable mistakes, keep adapting, keep strengthening the business and then – when you are absolutely sure that the business is in a sweet spot – step on the accelerator. He said what Rakesh Jhunjhunwala usually said, 'Make a mistake you can afford so that you live to make another one.'

Utpal suggested: why not test the market by selling products through modern retail format brands like Metro Shoes, Central, Shoppers Stop and Lifestyle. That way you would get precious consumer feedback for free. You wouldn't even have to move an inch; the retailer would be aggregating that feedback for us. Thereafter one can always scale with *fursat* (patience) with cash in the kitty. If you did it this way, you would be avoiding the trap of a high cap-ex, high op-ex, and high working capital retail business model.

I wasn't convinced. A consumer-facing company needed to own its customer to generate superior value. By what Utpal was suggesting, ours would be reduced to a mere distribution play. That would defeat the purpose of having got into business in the first place. I needed a direct control on my destiny, best achieved through a proprietary retail network. From where I stood and what I was imagining, I told Utpal that we needed more stores – not less. The demand was going to be huge. We had everything covered. I also agreed that in that spirit of 'more', we could add Metro, Central, Shoppers Stop and Lifestyle to our distribution footprint.

Utpal thought for a while. Then said: 'The challenge will lie in the execution. You can start your own stores, but that will stretch your fixed capital requirement. Besides, when you buy shoes from China by paying cash down, you would have already consumed your working capital. I have seen a number of good businesses destroyed – completely destroyed – because they had high fixed cap-ex coupled with high op-ex and high working capital intensity. Why I am worried for you is that you are loading too much pressure on the need to succeed early. If you don't deliver on the sales front immediately as you launch the business – and there is no saying when the brand may click, sometimes later rather than sooner – then... *you might not get another chance.*'

That sounded like a verdict being pronounced even before the action.

I came away feeling that Utpal had perhaps not grasped the import of the consumer proposition. World-class shoe.

Unbeatable price. Under-penetrated nation. Compelling endorsement. Supporting cash. How could we go wrong?

I had a different perspective of his working capital trap. When sales took off, we would place a second order and negotiate better credit terms from our Chinese suppliers. Several economies could moderate our break-even point. The fixed cost part of our business would get apportioned across higher sales. When operating leverage kicked in, profitability would rise. This initial squeeze was only a phase. Once revenues kicked in, it would be a virtuous cycle. He countered: what if the revenues don't match? The virtuous cycle could become a vicious cycle (explained below).

Utpal kept pushing me to see reality: 'If the shoes were retailed through established stores, you won't then need to invest on rents or fit-outs.'

My argument: The organized retail chains would carve away 30–40 per cent of the MRP as commission. They would not buy from us; they would only stock and pay when sold (or return). They sought a carte blanche to include our sports shoes as a part of their store discount schemes (the additional discount loaded on us). Each discounted pair would erode our brand.

'World-class joota koi paani ke bhaav mein bechega?' (Would anyone retail world-class shoes at throw-away prices?) I countered.

Utpal said, 'When we invested in companies, Prashant, do you remember the stocks where we lost the most money? Those were companies where we invested judging the upside and not factoring the risks. All I am saying is prepare for a downside scenario. Think, at least.'

I insisted, 'If I look at the downside, I will only see a downside. Seeing is believing. I don't want to walk that path. I feel confident. We have worked hard. We feel confident. I will add the department stores along with online as a strategy, but I want to go ahead aggressively with our proprietary retail model.'

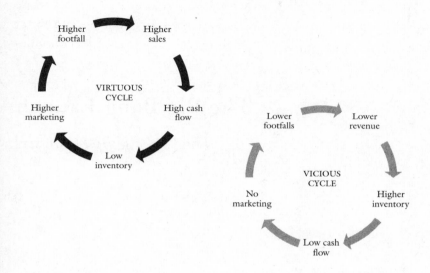

Virtuous Cycle Versus Vicious Cycle Explained

Utpal finally resigned. He said, 'Well, you know better.'

Before I left, Utpal made my day when he said, 'Prashant, I want to invest in your company. I want to back your conviction. Whatever you are comfortable with, but I am in as an investor.'

Utpal became a 5 per cent investor in D:FY.

20

The Big Bang Launch

How's the josh? High, sir!

21 August 2018.

Our debut at Phoenix Marketcity, Mumbai.

The big day had arrived. I walked into the mall at 8.00 a.m. As you enter Phoenix Marketcity, Kurla, from Entrance 2 (car entrance), you come across the escalator that takes you to the sports zone. As you descended, you could see the D:FY signage along with Adidas, Puma, Nike and Reebok. It was a proud moment. An Indian brand adjacent to the best. As you came down and took a right and entered the sports zone, the first store on your left was Puma, coloured red, and you had a Virat Kohli standee inside looking at you. The Puma store was large and stacked with merchandise. Opposite Puma was the Nike store. A large, sophisticated space with an international look marked by the prominent Nike Swoosh on the façade. The store looked subtle. Next to Nike was Adidas, the black Adidas façade with the three stripes in white; the images of Hima Das and Rohit Sharma observing all those walked past. The store looked international, and the Adidas Boost collection welcomed visitors. Next to it was the new 'cross fit' look Reebok Store. Masculine and gym-like with dumbbells and Shahid Kapoor's fit body and six packs embarrassing walkers. Amongst them stood D:FY. As large a store as Puma, Nike and Adidas. Bigger than Reebok. Better in presentation than global brands. The look of the store raw, grey and wired mesh on the façade with the D:FY logo in orange announcing a bold presence. Almost saying, *'Hum kisi se kam nahin'* (we are not inferior to anyone).

It was a proud moment. We had achieved in eighteen months what no other Indian brand had (M.S. Dhoni had started a sports brand called Seven and Mahesh Bhupati had started a sports brand called Zeven).

The store experience made heads turn. Early mall visitors were curiously awestruck. *'Kya dukaan hai ... chalo ek baar andar dekhte hain'* (What a store! Let's step inside once and take a look), I heard one say.

Hardik Pandya's image smiled down on prospective shoppers. Anil Kumble's images spoke about technology. We showcased the story of how we got there. Our technology. Our designs. Our designers. Our supply chain. Our partners. Our brand ambassadors.

Sure there were glitches. The agency appointed to create the D:FY brand video delivered something substandard. The store was only 75 per cent ready (looked like 100 per cent to visitors though). The signage was faulty.

However, we transformed the launch into an event. We engaged Harshad Chavan of Toast Events, India's biggest retail events company, to curate it. He relished my idea of a panel discussion on the day of launch amongst Kishore Biyani (on the viability of an Indian sports brand), Anil Kumble (on sport extending beyond cricket into India's mainstream), Ritesh Sidhwani and Farhan Akhtar (on why sports biopics were entering Indian cinema) and Mayank Shivam (Director, Amazon India, on sports category performance on e-commerce platforms) moderated by Mandira Bedi.

We had planned a temporary sports arena to be created next to the stage following the panel discussion. Harshad insisted that we would need celebrities to feature in the media. We engaged Rhea Chakraborty (fit, good-looking and female Hindi film star), Saqib Saleem (fit, six pack abs and a Hindi film background), Karan Tacker (fit, six pack abs and popular TV star) and Mandira Bedi. The result: our social media coverage generated a viewership of more than 100 million.

Harshad said, 'This is great. Let's make this bigger.' So we got influencers – Scarlet Johnson, Riaan George, Pranwesha, Abix, Juhi Godambe and others – in on the job.

We invited the print media, social media agencies, magazine editors, vendor partners, mall owners, friends and families. We flew Miro and Jeremy with their families down. We invited our China development and manufacturing partners as well.

At 11.00 a.m., we conducted a brief walking tour where the visitors interfaced with Kishore Biyani, Anil Kumble, Farhan Akhtar, Ritesh Sidhwani and Nidhhi Agerwal (Hardik Pandya was playing a Test match for India at Tunbridge Wells in England). We got the celebrities to select their shoes and t-shirt to wear for the store event.

When Kishore Biyani walked in, I kept a notepad handy. His verdict: 'You will sell more apparel than shoes. Shoes *mehenge lag rahe hain* (the shoes seem expensive). Your apparel is affordable and looks good. *Lekin itni badi dukaan kyon li ... Paagal ho?...*

Maroge.' (But why did you set up this big a store? Are you crazy? You'll land in trouble.) That apart, he asked who designed and executed the store (which I decoded as 'I approve'). Having been privy to how his face would crumple into a frown when he visited Big Bazaar and Central when things would not be right, I had been spared.

At noon, we trooped off for the panel discussion. We had an even bigger crowd waiting. The print, TV and digital media had descended. Before the panel discussion commenced, Kishore Biyani launched D:FY. We played the brand video (the substandard stuff) at the insistence of the agency because the launch provided it with an opportunity to showcase its work (I relented). Hardik came on 'live', shared his journey and wished us the best. Mandira invited Rajiv, Samir and me to the stage. I was in tears. Rajiv shared his thoughts. Samir spoke. Then the spotlight shifted to Kishore Biyani, Anil Kumble, Farhan Akhtar, Ritesh Sidhwani and Mayank Shivam.

When the panel discussion concluded and the celebrities dispersed, the second round (Rhea, Saqib, Nidhhi, Mandira and Karan Tacker) commenced. First, they would walk wearing our 'walking' range of shoes. They would sprint (wearing Brooks). They would play cricket, hockey and soccer (wearing multi-sport shoes). They would enter the gym area and work out three sets (in our gym range of shoes) to a cheering assemblage and loud music.

My friend Sandeep Gupta had flown from Singapore for this event. He joined late; I took him around the store (coincidentally, one afternoon, chatting about this opportunity at his house in Singapore, I had resolved to explore D:FY). As we came down the escalator, the store was jam-packed. There were customers after customers (friends and family included) trying the shoes and apparel. There was a queue at the cash counter. We had started manual billing since we had only two POS machines. There was a big queue outside the trial room. In all this chaos, we had online influencers taking pictures and videos for Instagram, Facebook and YouTube. The store buzz energy was something else. As I took Sandeep through the store, visitors congratulated me (friends and family). My cousins who had flown in from Vadodara and Rajkot were clicking pictures with celebrities and influencers. Chetan, my friend from Kolkata, who was down with his son, Abhi, pulled me aside, hugged me and started crying. Chetan had been a witness to my financially stressed existence in Kolkata. He reminded me how we did not go to a dandiya (Indian folk dance) night in Kolkata because we could not muster Rs 20 in entry fees. Sandeep, a person of few words, gave me a thumbs up.

My close friends Kavish (from Kolkata) and Ashish – also investors in D:FY – were standing in the queue for check-out with several products. 'Seth, mind blowing,' said Kavish with a proud smile and a salute.

That event cost Rs 45 lakh. To compensate, our revenue crossed Rs 8,00,000 that day.

It validated my optimism on the size of the market, quality of shoes and our mall-driven approach. I carried the 'I always told you' look for days.

It was to be the highest we would sell in any of our stores … *in any month*.

21

Launch Conversations

Kuch inki suno

Over the next two months, I attended a number of panel discussions and was a speaker in some as well. Ever since we conceptualized the launch event, the panel discussion was something I had looked forward to.

Given the line-up, Rajiv and I concluded that we could not be part of this since our achievements (mine more than his) were negligible compared to the panellists.

Kishore Biyani had redefined India's modern retail sector and had been credited with the title of Raja of Indian Retail.

Anil Kumble was the highest wicket-taker for India and coach of the Indian cricket team. The two most moving images of him: bowling with a bandaged jaw (taking the wicket of Brain Lara) and his 10/74 against Pakistan, only the second bowler in all of Test history to take ten wickets in an innings.

Farhan Akhtar, director, actor, singer, producer, poet, lyricist, writer. His *Dil Chahta Hai*, a cult film, introduced India to GenX. His transformation and performance in *Bhaag Milkha Bhaag* inspired the comment, 'Is that really him?'

Ritesh Sidhwani, the producer and pillar behind Excel Entertainment, delivered memorable content through films like *Dil Chahta Hai*, *Rock On*, *Don* and *Don 2*, *Dil Dhadakne Do*, *Zindagi Na Milegi Dobara*, *Gold*, *Gully Boy*, *Fukrey* and more.

Mayank Shivam, Director at Amazon.

The stage was set. The panellists were welcomed. The picture appeared like a dream film sequence. These achievers were now commenting on a business that had not even been conceived eighteen months ago. I chose to stand in a corner and listen.

Kishore Biyani

Kishore Biyani spoke on how sports had always been a part of Indian heritage, whether it was *gilli danda* (a game using a long stick to hit a piece of sharpened wood) or cricket or football. He spoke about some businesses being built around sport, commercial activity woven around sport through clothing, footwear, TV and advertising. That celebrities and star were created from sports in a big way. 'Sports is taking a new turn, and will grow and grow and grow,' he said.

He turned to D:FY. 'What I have seen in the way D:FY has been conceptualized is that there is always a gap between what is available and what is required. D:FY has tried to address this gap through product and pricing. Once you get into business, it's an entrepreneurial journey. It is learning while doing.'

Kishore Biyani spoke of the first Pantaloons store in Kolkata and how he had learned on the way. That they got it right on the first instance. He said that the customer would respond;

we needed to learn and respond. He also mentioned that the initial concept and positioning had been executed well by us. And finally, he joked about two *Gujju* (abbreviated word for Gujaratis) entrepreneurs starting out.

Kishore Biyani also passed a view on our aggression: opening twenty-two stores in nine cities. 'Entrepreneurship is all about risk. It seems like a reasonable risk to me.' He gave us credit for thinking big. He cautioned that sports was a risky category as we would be dealing with variables of sizes, SKUs, fashion, time-to-market, etc. He also mentioned that he had never taken a risk of such magnitude in 'this' category. Then he smiled and made our day when he said, 'I will learn to take some risk from Rajiv and Prashant now.' Everyone applauded.

When he was asked what advice he would give D:FY, he said it would make sense to first build the brand. He asked us to emotionally connect with the consumer. He said that the surprise would come from Plan B – apparel and not footwear. 'Apparel will be 60–70 per cent of D:FY's business,' he predicted.

Anil Kumble

Anil Kumble spoke on how sports was expanding beyond cricket. 'It is not just about cricket any more. There are other sports. We are growing as a sporting nation. We are performing better at the international level. We now have icons beyond cricket.'

Kumble spoke of how India had graduated from watching sports to playing sports. You could now see people walking, running and cycling despite growing distractions. He spoke about why he selected to partner D:FY. 'Companies like D:FY are helping by providing quality sports gear,' he said.

He added how emotionally invested we were in D:FY. He said that his involvement extended beyond the brand. He mentioned that sports was now a lifestyle statement for youth where it extended beyond comfort to appearance, adding along the way that the right attire and shoes prevented injuries. He indicated that D:FY addressed all of these realities; that 'India has many aspirational brands, and all we needed was an affordable one.'

Kumble emphasized the affordability attribute. He said not everyone could afford expensive shoes in India. And just because you cannot afford, you cannot be using the same shoe for long as it affects performance. That is where affordable pricing cum quality came in. He said that D:FY ticked all the boxes.

Farhan Akhtar

Farhan Akhtar put on his celluloid glasses. He spoke on sports in cinema and cinema in sports. Story-telling through sports had entered mainstream Bollywood. There was a lot for the audience to learn about character, failure, failure management, motivation from sports. Because essentially stories from sports were easy to comprehend.

Farhan communicated his impressions about us. 'I am personally glad they have chosen to open stores where people can touch and feel sports gear, wear the shoes, move around.' For him, see–touch–feel was an important part of the experience of any new brand. When you get used to the philosophy of the brand and the way it fits you, then being relaxed and ordering online would become simpler.

Farhan also spoke on product design. 'In everything we do, aesthetics plays an important role. From the moment we met them at our office, and they opened the suitcase, there were 25–30 different pairs of shoes, which captured my eye.' He added: 'I wanted to hold them, try them all as they looked amazingly cool. They are not just great shoes, but great-looking as well. It is about time that we had a true Indian brand that can represent all these aspirations of Indian youth entering sport,' he said with pride, showing off the D:FY bright yellow shoe he was wearing.

Ritesh Sidhwani

Ritesh, like Farhan, begins his day with kickboxing. He spoke about his emotions connected with workouts. He spoke on his decision to invest in D:FY. 'I met Rajiv and Prashant by chance, heard their story and conviction in D:FY. More than investing in the brand, Farhan and I are investing in them.'

Ritesh also found D:FY to be the right product that addressed the right market gap. He spoke of how his sons and he were sneaker freaks and would shop for sneakers when travelling abroad. He said that when he tried D:FY shoes, he felt good about wearing them. 'When I wore D:FY, I loved them and I am going to keep wearing them. You will see me in D:FY often. I have left what I was wearing behind.'

Mayank Shivam

Mayank spoke about sports as a category on Amazon. 'Sports is clearly one of the largest emerging categories at Amazon,' he said. He elaborated the need for more brands and wider choice that would grow the market. He indicated that brands like D:FY were taking a bold step and that demand would emerge from Tier-2 and Tier-3 towns. The role of Amazon would be to take D:FY to the real India. 'D:FY is at the cusp of something big. We would love to partner D:FY and be a part of its journey,' he said.

He spoke about Amazon's meeting us. 'The first time I met Rajiv and Prashant we were inspired by their research and effort. Being runners, both understood the challenges faced by many like them – and addressed them,' he said. The outcome was an exclusive Amazon partnership. 'We have confidence in D:FY, which has a large role to play in making quality sports gear affordable for India,' he concluded.

The 45-minute discussion passed by like a few minutes. That night I remembered my father and my late friend Aalok. My eyes misted. I missed their presence. An unconfident child from Kolkata had dared to build a truly Indian sports brand.

THE DEFEAT

22

What's the Hurry?

Itni bhi kya jaldi hai

By the time we were some months into D:FY's existence, one reality was becoming evident. We were trying too much too fast.

Much of this could be ascribed to the baggage I had brought to the business.

When I was young, I had grown up on success stories: of a relative who had gone from scratch to wealth; of a businessperson who had set up companies that employed thousands; of Dhirubhai Ambani who had redefined what it was to be successful in a pre-liberalization India; of Rakesh Jhunjhunwala who had grown his seed investable capital thousands of times over.

I remembered that I had once recommended an investment in Kirloskar Brothers to Rakesh Jhunjhunwala. He bought stock; it appreciated in a few months. A few months later, I reminded him of my recommendation. He asked: 'How many shares did you buy?' I said: 'Two hundred'. He quoted George Soros. 'It doesn't matter whether you are right or wrong. What matters is how much money you made when you were right and how much money you lost when you were wrong.'

When I launched D:FY, it wasn't just important to launch a successful sports brand; it was important how much money we made if we got it right. The benchmark was *always* money. There was nothing wrong with our 'no compromise' approach; however, this approach sucked us into a mindset that would perhaps have been compatible for a larger company.

For instance, we didn't want to start small. When we ordered 34,000 pairs of shoes and 1,00,000 garments in the opening season, we estimated we would liquidate 80 per cent in the first six months. That worked out to a sales throughput of approximately 200 pairs of footwear a day and 600 garment units. In turn, that worked out to ten pairs a day per store (based on an outlay of twenty stores) in addition to what we could generate online. That worked out to selling one pair per hour per store. When one considered the vastness of the market, the preference for sports shoes, our product quality and attractive price positioning, if there was anything that we could not be accused of, it was conservatism.

So when we were ordering for the first time from China, I shook my head. We were ordering too low.

At every stage, my perspective revealed a distinct urgency.

The Future Group versus DMart Story As I See It (The Rabbit and the Hare)

In most success stories, perhaps the most underappreciated attribute is patience.

Future Group (FG) launched its first Big Bazaar in Hyderabad in 2001; Avenue Supermarkets launched its first DMart in Powai, Mumbai, in 2002. The Big Bazaar focus was fashion (food and general merchandise); D-Mart's focus was grocery (general merchandise and not fashion).

In ten years, Big Bazaar grew to 250 stores; DMart grew patiently to a mere ten stores. Big Bazaar had a lead of 200+ stores over DMart. Meanwhile, as FG used its capital in expanding a working-capital-intensive store network across all parts of India and in marketing to generate additional footfall, DMart used its capital to buy properties and set up an easy pace to store growth. DMart focused on inventory turns (food and grocery generating the highest). At FG, our inventory turns were 4x (because of fashion products that moved relatively slower); at DMart it was 16x (because food moved faster). We paid for rent; they did not. We used debt to grow; DMart had surplus capital and used equity. FG invested in its store ambience; DMart invested in no-frills stores with basic air-conditioning. Interestingly, every penny saved was offered to the customer through the lowest prices (strengthening the 'Every Day Low Prices' positioning).

One visible reality separated the two companies. FG was in a hurry (rabbit); DMart wasn't (hare).

Interestingly, over the next seven years, Big Bazaar opened fifty stores; DMart launched 190 stores in the next decade.

Only when the model had been perfected did DMart step on the accelerator.

As on January 2021, DMart enjoyed a market capitalization of Rs 1,80,000 crore. As a result of the debt burden and trap (accelerated by COVID-19 and lower sales), Future Group lost the plot and sold out to Reliance Retail. The hare won. Hands down.

At D:FY, even as I had studied this story well, the import was lost on me.

We planned beyond our bandwidth; we spent beyond budget; we expanded beyond means.

The promoters (mostly) brought Rs 25 crore into the business. Rs 10 crore was invested in fixed assets, Rs 10 crore in working capital and Rs 5 crore in brand building and op-ex (rent, electricity, people cost). At peak, we had nearly 90 people working with us; we had offices in two cities.

We were preparing for a marathon like a 100 metre sprint.

When we went into business, we felt that an investment outlay of nearly Rs 20 crore would keep us in business forever.

Our 2018 Diwali campaign had commenced. Hoardings across Mumbai and Bengaluru were impressive. The festivities had begun at people's homes. I was praying that the sentiment would extend to our stores as well.

23

Diwali Campaign

Band baaja ... par baaraat kahaan?

O ne of the earliest dilemmas that we faced was whether we should first build the D:FY brand first or the business first.

When one is building a brand, one is essentially building a recall. It takes years to carve out recall in a world marked by clutter. Only after significant upfront investments and extensive brand sustenance, when the brand salience has been established, does the brand translate into higher consumer walk-ins, premium pricing, quicker offtake and recall longevity. This requires significant investment upfront.

On the other hand, when one builds a business, one invests in the product, pricing, people, quality, logistics, distribution, credit and working capital availability. Gradually, as the oiled mechanics begin to move smoother, the business begins to generate a progressively larger surplus that is then reinvested, and then – only then – the brand investment is emphasized. Interestingly, this warrants a lower upfront investment.

If there was one reason why successful brand creation had become increasingly challenging, it was media expansion. If one invested in print, there was a possibility that a section of consumers only visited online formats. If one invested only in the online, there was a missed opportunity in outdoor media. If one invested only in the outdoor media, there was the possibility of a gaping hole when it came to print. If one invested in radio or Spotify or gaana.com, there was always the possibility that one addressed only that consumer.

The second challenge was India's demographic dividend story. Every consumer and consumer-technology brand sought to 'acquire' the Indian consumer. Global brands, Indian brands, consumer-tech businesses, insurance companies and gaming companies, among others, all desired a share. All possessed large budgets. The Indian media was in demand, and expensive.

At D:FY, we had factored most costs into account. However, the largest expense head we had *underestimated* was media spend. I asked a prominent brand management agency what one should do with a budget of Rs 2 crore. He countered, 'That's it?' He then added: 'Only impact advertising'. This meant that we should focus on just Mumbai and Bengaluru for fifteen days and flood those cities with hoardings, circumvent print media and invest in digital promotion … and then wait for shoes to move off our shelves.

When the seduction waned and if we sold only a few hundred shoes during the fortnight, we would have to troop wearily back to the first square: find more cash to generate more sales. 'Buy sales' would have been more appropriate.

The magnitude of the error began to dawn on us. We had invested in a high capital expenditure-upfront business model with absolutely no sales assurance. We had been carried away by the power of our optimism to have overlooked two of the most important words in any business scenario: 'Worst case'.

As an analyst, one was taught sensitivity analysis. One put assumptions to test for the best case and worst-case deviation from the mean (normal case or realistic case). The best case involved everything going better than planned where revenues grew higher than expected and costs remained the same, resulting in a positive operating leverage* where profits grew faster and higher than estimated. In the worst-case scenario revenues under-performed the normal case and with costs remaining fixed, a negative operating leverage would begin to kick in where profits nosedived, and you reported a loss. Based on the gap (best case minus worse case), you adapted the cost structure. If the gap was not high, you generally let things be, but if they were high, you altered the business model and fixed costs. This analysis sensitized one to risks. As an analyst, one could always ignore the best case and settle for something between the worst case and the normal. If that appealed, we recommended the stock.

In our brand-led business model, the cost was high. You spent ahead of performance and awaited the outcome. We were confident; ours would fall between the normal and best case; the worst case was simply never considered.

We desired to build a sports brand. We opted for a brand-led business model even though we had moderate capital. The challenge lay within: we felt the brand could be built instantly.

We selected to work with Grey Worldwide as our creative agency.

Grey Worldwide attended the final pitch with creatives as they would appear on hoardings, bus shelters and inside the stores and malls (as we had asked). Besides, Grey pitched for our digital account and product packaging opportunity.

We needed a still photo shoot of our brand ambassadors for the hoardings, print ads and visual merchandizing inside our stores. We needed to make videos with them for digital marketing and the social media. We needed a brand video for the launch (indicated earlier). 'How much will the still and video shoot cost?' I asked.

'One crore,' they said. I felt I might have heard wrong.

The cost of photography during the eight hours allocated by Hardik Pandya across two days and a day with Anil Kumble were priced at Rs 15 lakh a day. The video shoots would require a director, videographer, post-production studio hand, musician, extras, hair stylist and fashion stylist. I countered with a budget of Rs 30 lakh. Grey suggested, 'Then stick with the stills and let us eliminate the videos.' So we engaged a different video content creation agency.

We were spending Rs 2.10 crore on the agencies and brand ambassadors to be able to invest Rs 1.5 crore on our advertising.

Crazy.

Heads	Investments (Rs)
Brand ambassadors	10,000,000
Brand consulting	2,500,000
Ad-agency retainers	4,000,000
Photoshoots	4,500,000
Total	21,000,000

Big brands and companies spend significantly on brand ambassadors, stills and photo shoots. However, they invest in multiples on advertising to leverage this spend. If Pepsi, say, pays Rs 15 crore to Salman Khan, it will spend Rs 150 crore on ensuring that everyone knows that Salman Khan drinks Pepsi. The ratio should have been 5x to 20 x to 50x for us; it was 0.67x. *Chai se zyada ketli garam thhi* (the kettle proved hotter than the tea).

After Grey's creatives had been screened, I needed an endorsement from Kishore Biyani. Over the years, one had seen him make subtle alterations in Big Bazaar's creatives that enhanced the consumer connect. As a spin-off benefit, I felt that there was an outside possibility that he could, after seeing our creatives, get interested enough to tell me, *'Kuch equity dene ke liye ho toh bataana ...'* (If you are raising capital, let me know).

I extracted the board-backed print of the creative prepared by Grey. I placed it in front of him. I stepped back with the glow of the man stepping out with a newborn to be shown to the grandparents.

Kishore Biyani's reaction: *'Yeh kya kar rahe ho,* Prashant?' (What are you doing?)

I could have been pushed over by a feather.

'Kyun (Why?) Kishoreji? Where is the problem?'

'Problem?!' he thundered. *'Sab kuch galat hai. Baat karte ho jootey ki aur dikhaate ho sirf Hardik Pandya!'* (Everything is wrong. You are talking about shoes and only showcasing Hardik Pandya!)'

'But Kishoreji, we are not selling a shoe but a concept,' I interrupted.

'Sawaal hi nahi hai!' (No way!) he thundered. *'Tumhara champion joota hai. Joote mein kahaani hai. Aur uska naam-o-nishaan nahi!'* (Your shoe is your champion. Your shoe has a story. And it is invisible in the advertisement!)

Kishore Biyani called Santosh Desai. 'Santosh?! I have seen the D:FY campaign with Hardik Pandya. It needs a complete re-think and re-design. Complete!'

I had gone expecting India's Mr Modern Retail man to say *'Shabaash* (brilliant), Prashant! Let's make this big together. Bring D:FY into Future Group.'

On the contrary, he was asking me to turn to the drawing board and tell Grey Worldwide, 'Sorry, we may have all liked it but Kishore Biyani has a different take on it, so can we do this all over again?'

Grey Worldwide went back, reworked the campaign and brought the shoe upfront to make it the 'hero'.

Worse was in store.

We had entered into an exclusive e-commerce partnership with Amazon. In exchange for this exclusivity, Amazon had offered to pick up the tab for 25 per cent of our marketing spend with a provision: it would pay only after it had approved our promotional campaign. We showed the reworked creatives (after Kishore Biyani's inputs) to Amazon. Amazon liked the campaign, but not the punchline. 'All we want is to focus on affordability and comfort in the ad copy in a large font size,' Amazon demanded.

The campaign was again redone. The result is what we eventually carried did not carry a word of emotion, brand, pitch, unaided recall, pride or Indianness.

Every rupee of what we had spent on the brand strategy and positioning with Future Brands had disappeared down the tube.

All of Rs 25 lakh. Some 15 per cent of our brand spend had yielded nothing.

GREY CAMPAIGN

APPROVED BY KISHORE BIYANI   FINAL CAMPAIGN

Once we had hesitatingly agreed on the final campaign, we chose the Diwali Week 2018 to launch D:FY. We chose to spend aggressively in Mumbai and Bengaluru since we had ten stores of seventeen in those cities. We invested in hoardings in prime locations. We invested in bus shelters to enhance street visibility. We invested in radio jingles. We enhanced advertising inside malls. We were on Facebook, Google, YouTube and timesofindia.com. Along with Amazon, we budgeted to spend Rs 2 crore.

And yet after the Rs 2 crore spend, we did not see any revenue uptick. We would see our neighbours (Nike, Adidas and Skechers) buzzing; we were struggling.

The campaign had not stirred any water; all the work in making Hardik Pandya the face of our product and getting Grey Worldwide, Kishore Biyani and Amazon to the table … we had passed like a ship on a moonless night with the lights switched off.

*Operating leverage explained

The sensitivity of profit to changes in revenue. A measure of fixed operating cost intensity in the business. Retail has a high fixed cost; operating leverage is high. The problem is it cuts both ways.

Retail Model (Rs)	Break Even Revenue	Revenues Up by 50%	Revenues Down by 50%
Revenues	725,000	1,087,500	362,500
Rent & Maintenance	500,000	500,000	500,000
Electricity	75,000	75,000	75,000
Employee	100,000	100,000	100,000
Others	50,000	50,000	50,000
Store operating costs	725,000	725,000	725,000
Store Profit	–	362,500	–362,500

In a retail business, revenue sensitivity is key. If more customers buy, you generate disproportionate cash flows and vice versa.

24

Team

Satth sudharahi satth sangati paayi

When I embarked on the dream to build India's truly sports brand, there was a growing recognition that we would only be as good as the people who worked with us. This is what I had seen at Future Group, FT and other organizations.

There were two perspectives: recruit 'unknown' professionals based on a specific competence (gap in the organization); or recruit 'known' executives one was familiar with and allow them to learn on the job.

Both options can be argued: if one hired purely by identifying the competence gap and then recruiting professionals (even better than oneself), then their complementary capabilities would bring diverse skills that could only strengthen our company. On the other hand, such professionals would come at a high cost, would have high autonomy expectations and, worse, could possibly expose us as being inadequately equipped to address the sectorial opportunity. Besides, how did one trust them? We had no reference point since we had never worked with them.

On the other hand, if one hired 'known' talent even as that 'known' would not be immediately competent, the person would be affordable, temperamentally manageable, would not rock the boat and was more likely to merge in from day one. Besides, one would never have to second-guess intent and motivation.

We selected the latter option: the known.

The person I turned to was Samir Saraiya, who I had worked with at Future Group for 12+ years. Samir lived in the same building as mine in Kolkata. We had spent our childhood together across fifteen years; we had lived virtually in each other's homes. When he expressed an interest in joining D:FY, I turned the knobs on. I could have asked, 'What skills will you bring to the table?' On the contrary, I wooed Samir into the company by dropping lines like, 'Samir, it's time to create wealth for yourself, and for that, I believe, I have the perfect platform.' If we succeeded, I told him, he would be far better off than in Future Group.

I didn't have to 'sell' D:FY to Samir. He trusted. Besides, he too was looking at a quasi-entrepreneurial journey. He resigned even before our company was formally registered.

Samir had one thing going for him. He was the most hard-working person at D:FY. He was a good executor. He could execute what he was told in an area where he possessed experience. He could take an initiative from point A to point B; he could be my pulse on the business; he could pick up the threads that I left for him and report to me in a few days. He was like my chief-of-staff.

Samir got the same remuneration at D:FY that he earned at Future Group; he also got 5 per cent sweat equity that would enable him to create wealth over time; he was to be stationed in Mumbai but could travel to Kolkata to meet his family whenever he wished.

When I needed another hand, I turned to my brother Ketan whose previous engagement had been in the capacity of a financial communicator. His principal credential: he was my brother. He would come at no cost to the company (promoter's brother where my equity ownership would be shared with him). He was frugal. I asked him to handle our e-commerce and supply chain functions. Even as Ketan had never managed these functions in the past, there was nothing complicated that could not be mastered.

These decisions were to come back to bite us at a later day.

The Mistake that Delayed Rs 4 Crore

For months I lived a dream of bringing to India a sports brand that that would make Indians proud.

Within a month of our shoes being launched in retail stores, I began to realize that something was amiss.

Not just with the shoe. With ourselves.

The story: We launched D:FY on Prime Day at Amazon on 16 July 2018. This was well before we launched D:FY retail stores. This then was to be the first time that we showcased our dream brand to the Indian consumers. As per the prevailing arrangement, our supply chain vendor was required to transport directly to Cloudtail (CT), the seller of our products on Amazon. CT operated through a portal, no physical intervention. Its system was paperless: CT placed an indent for 'x' number of shoes, we downloaded the list, we approved the list, the system generated a purchase order, and the portal generated a time slot of where and at what time to deliver. Once the product was accepted at the CT-directed warehouse they paid us in forty-five days (after deducting commission) since they purchased it from us.

Besides the Prime Day quantities, we were required to deliver to CT the full order by the first week of August 2018 and expected to be reimbursed by mid-September.

Mid-September came. I asked Anirudh (chief financial officer) whether CT had credited Rs 4 crore to our account. He checked the portal. The portal indicated cryptically: 'Not due'.

'What do they mean by "not due"?' I demanded. We checked. Then rechecked. We discovered: our first consignment of sports shoes, apparel and accessories had not yet been delivered to CT's warehouse.

Not. Delivered. Yet.

Gradually the story tumbled out: our trucker had delayed in reaching the indicated warehouse and lost the allotted time-slot, making it imperative to reapply for a delivery time-slot; the second warehouse where we needed to deliver in early August refused to accept the consignment for an unknown reason; when our transporter asked for a revised delivery slot, he was told that the CT warehouse slot was heavily booked and new slots would be allotted later. The transporter relayed this to Samir (who was handling the function).

Samir did not relay to us.

The delay was never escalated. Our products continued to languish in vehicles in Delhi in the open (sun affects the glue that is used to bind the midsole with the upper). A cash inflow of Rs 4 crore was being criminally delayed.

This is where we recognized that as a team we did not possess the processes for timely communication. There was no review meeting everyday where such challenges could be shared or acted upon. Because there was so much going on due to all of us doing varied things, we assumed that everyone was doing what they were supposed to. Besides, if there ever were to be an issue, we would be immediately informed, we *assumed* and *expected*. This led to people doing what they thought was best according to them, but not according to what would be best for the organization.

After a series of discussions with Samir, Team CT and our logistics partner, our maiden delivery reached CT warehouses in late September 2018. The interest cost on the delay of nearly fifty days amounted to Rs 12 lakh – the equivalent of 400 pairs of sales. Gone. Just like that.

The excuses were plenty: everything was systems-led so Samir did not know how our intervention would have produced a different result; besides, he said that we were so busy with the D:FY launch that he didn't want to consume my time. Intent was right, inaction not so.

Professional and Personal Cocktail

D:FY was top-heavy from the outset.

Five of the eight people who had joined in the first few months were seniors and we took this reality to a level of chaos.

My brother Ketan who had been recruited for the business and transferred to Bengaluru to manage the supply chain and e-commerce functions shared residential space with Samir to moderate expenses; he would lunch at the residence of my co-promoter Rajiv Mehta. The lady who joined as our visual merchandizer resided in Mumbai but attended to her Bengaluru responsibilities long-distance. Rajiv's management style was hands-off and despite handling retail he would not periodically visit our stores but conduct business review meetings from office. Mine was a completely hands-on approach where I would aggregate inputs on everything, irrespective of my direct responsibility and expertise. My ego was always presented upfront: I would expect people to assume my point of view. I was the founder, after all.

When dissenting opinions were expressed, my ego would be offended.

When things wouldn't go as I planned, I would simmer at work; then the simmer would bubble.

Besides, the professional and personal kept overlapping.

The web of inter-connected relationships made it increasingly difficult for Rajiv, Samir and Ketan to raise professional issues because at some point Ketan was beholden that my family would be hosting everyone for lunch every day in Mumbai. Even when they desired to communicate to me that there were mismatches between expectations and reality, one stopped after a point because after all I was 'family'. The same applied to them as well.

There were blunders all around. We underperformed across product perception, retail sales, online sales, marketing, social media, supply chain, accounting and finance. Instead of errors being highlighted, the personal prevailed over the professional with concessions being made for 'What if Prashant feels bad? Do I have the right to interfere in his domain? He is like family after all.'

Besides, the difference in management styles – mine being hands-on and Rajiv's being largely hands-off – became increasingly visible. Each time I did a round of our retail stores – the gateway that would attract consumers, generate cash flows and strengthen our valuation – I would come back with points that I needed to raise with Rajiv. I would not be happy with the way some product would not be available due to size issues. My immediate response would be to call Rajiv from the retail outlet. His reply would be standard, in fact so standard that after a time

I began to predict what he was going to tell me. ('It happens, so let me check with Sudhakar and get back to you.')

Rajiv faced similar challenges with me. When it came to my marketing slippages, Rajiv should have blown the top and showed me the mirror. But because our management styles were so different he glossed over them.

There were no roles or responsibilities that had ever been defined. The result: gaps everywhere.

Our Mumbai branch was a store-cum-office. Store of 850 sq ft and 500 sq ft of office. And I sat there, with my ego and anger.

Our warehouse would also be adequately stocked with sports shoes of all SKUs, but in the Mumbai office-store consumers would ask for specific sizes or colours and we would be compelled to tell them, 'Sorry, we don't have it immediately in stock but if you could come in a day or two, we will get it for you.' We were staring at a last-mile issue: the consumer was actually asking for our product and we did not have it on our shelves or in the back room. It was like the marathoner tripping on the laces at the last kilometre.

In the business of retail, inventory management is an art and science. Inventory is Purchase minus Sale. One needs to forecast what one will sell even before one has purchased. This was art. In addition to research and retrospective data, inventory forecasting warrants a gut-feel-based reading of market demand. In our case, we did not possess any retrospective data, so everything boiled down to our gut-feel. The problem was that our gut was never *just positive* but *hugely positive*. The result was that we inevitably concluded that we would be able to sell the most in the least time – all the time. In line with this estimation, our inventory would be ordered.

Inventory was now a function of how much we sold versus how much we bought. Sale was demand fulfilment. Demand fulfilment was pure science. This is where the stock replenishment policy came in. We ended up being wrong on our gut (forecast), and where we were right, we couldn't book all the sales we should have because our science was not up to the mark.

We had set the business up all right; we didn't know how to get it going. We had recruited for familiarity, not knowledge. We didn't have one leak; we had a series of leaks transpiring concurrently and paying for it.

It was time for course-correction.

Nothing Going Right

Even though it had been only three months in business, sales were sluggish, inventory high and cash flows weak.

The team agreed that *Jo bhi karo lekin maal becho!* (Do what you have to, but sell!)

There were three engines at D:FY – sales, supply chain and product (design, development and sourcing). We decided that Rajiv, Ketan and I (with Samir being brought back to Mumbai) would push sales (and generate cash flows). Ketan would also address supply chain management. Now what we needed was someone to take the product portfolio off us and run with it for the second season.

This time we made a change in our recruitment approach; we went for knowledge and competence. Rajiv said he had someone just in mind for us. His ex-colleague Amit Kumar (real name withheld), sourcing head at Arvind Fashions for footwear and apparel.

I oozed my helicopter vision when we pitched to Amit. He was expensive. We had to think differently to have him onboard.

Once again, rather than asking him what he brought to the table and how would he help D:FY on the product side, I started over-selling D:FY to Amit.

'We have a vision to change the way sports shoes and apparel are made and sold in this country.'

'We don't just seek to make a surplus. We wish to create wealth.'

'Enough of working for someone else. This is where you work for the future of your family.'

'We aren't just a business. We are "family".'

'Besides salary, take home sweat equity based on deliverables.'

'This could be your big break in life. Take risks and rewards shall follow.'

Amit Kumar, who had previously worked with global and Indian fashion retailers and earned a seven-figure remuneration, surprised us when he said yes. He would condescend to join D:FY.

A part of his key result area was that Amit would help us moderate cost of procurement (10 per cent reduction was the target we outlined). Even before he had joined, he moderated this by 3 per cent by taking the phone and speaking to our China agent (whom he had recommended we source from).

We had recruited a rock star. Through the savings, Amit had reduced the net impact of his remuneration by Rs 30 lakh (if we placed a similar Rs 10 crore order for a second season). This was before he joined us.

Gradually, a different picture began to emerge. This became visible when we were working on a project to be enlisted as the sports gear partner of Jaipur Pink Panthers, Abhishek Bachchan's professional kabaddi team. The agreement was based on a barter. We would get to put our logo on their team merchandise and use team JPP images for our social media promotions. In return, we would be required to provide the kit for the team as well as jerseys for the family and friends of the Bachchans.

We entrusted the execution of this project to Amit.

Amit, our sourcing head, insisted that we work through vendors in Ludhiana he was familiar with. We encouraged him to lead. We gave him complete autonomy (and trusted him). The Bachchan family expectations were high.

However, there were issues after issues after issues:

- An issue with the logo size on the vests. *Not acceptable to JPP.*
- Names of players were spelt wrong. *Completely unacceptable to JPP.*
- Colour shades did not match. *Not acceptable to JPP.*
- Logos of sponsors were positioned wrongly. *A blunder.*

JPP too kept changing its brief. The delivery of the T-shirts was delayed. Each time JPP called, it fired the hell out of me; I would turn the cannon inwards on Amit.

Amit was used to working in a large corporation with a large team. He was used to driving sourcing strategically and the team doing the heavy lifting. He was there to negotiate with vendors and take strategic calls. In a start-up like ours, this luxury didn't exist. Amit had not gauged this trade-off. One evening, in Ludhiana, Amit collapsed and was hospitalized. The job had got to him. He quit soon after.

Samir was dispatched to Ludhiana on the next flight. He called within hours of reaching. 'Prashant, the production facility is not even sub-standard. It's a shed with only a few *kaarigar*s (workers).'

Total disaster.

25

Financial Blunders

Khayaali pulao

The one area where I floundered big time was finance.

Finance touches every function and yet it was the one capability at which we – I more than anyone – cut a sorry figure. The understanding required nothing more complex than an MS Excel spreadsheet and some common sense.

The one area where I inexcusably faltered was an excessive decision-making dependence on hurried (often mistaken) back-of-the-envelope calculations, an irony coming from someone who had stood fourth all India in the CWA examination and was a CA and a stock-picking analyst.

Take something as simple as the landed delivered cost of the sports shoe.

The FOB value of the sports shoe needed to be multiplied by 1.2x to arrive at the post-customs duty (20 per cent) landed price. Thereafter, one added 18 per cent GST. Plus, clearing charges. Plus, insurance. Plus, storage.

The multi-step increases in the delivered cost of the shoe meant that if the FOB was 100 in China, the landed price would be 1.68 by the time it reached our warehouse.

The general response in the sports shoe business – as possibly in most retail businesses – is to multiply the landed price by 3–4x to arrive at the price at which needed to be retailed. And here the reality of our error began to become evident.

When I had done my usual back-of-the-envelope calculation of the cost of an imported sports shoe while standing in the middle of the excitement of the Canton Fair, one had added just the 20 per cent to their FOB price ($8–9) and arrived at the landed cost; when multiplied by 4, one got a price of around 1.48x or Rs 3,000 for the best shoe on offer that we felt was ready to carve away mid-market share from the Nikes of the world. When we now arrived at the same calculation after factoring a few intermediate cost-adds (freight, insurance, GST to be added on post import duty cost and not on FOB) that we had missed, the end price was Rs 4,000 – 33 per cent higher.

The game had changed. No, it had reversed.

The whole advantage we intended to carve hinged on a perceptible price difference between D:FY and established global brands like Nike, Adidas, Puma etc. This had been diluted. Our competitive advantage took a large step backwards. ANTA succeeded because there was a perceived difference between Nike and Adidas not just in terms of price but in terms of value. This was critical as the entire business model rested on this hypothesis.

This had changed. *So should we have.*

Rather than redrawing the map and asking whether it was at all possible to fight the battle from a suddenly changed vantage point, we rallied more out of misplaced confidence than knowledge.

'We will figure this out,' I said. 'Either we will negotiate better against larger volumes or we will move to a lower price and lower margin in the first season. Besides, we will also have GST input credit,' I said to myself.

I had seen the new world. I had drunk the heady wine of the Canton Fair. I had penetrated the deep recesses of Jinjiang.

I could be deferred; I could be delayed; I could not be distracted, leaning on the famous stock market mantra that 'All bull markets climb a wall of worry.'

Touché.

Back of the envelope	
FOB Price of Shoes from China	100
Import Duty	20
GST	18
	138
Retail Multiple	4
Selling Price	552
Actual calculation	
FOB Price of Shoes from China	100
Freight, incurance and other expenses	12.15
Cost for calculation of import duty	112.15
Importy Duty: 20% + 10% Cess	24.75
Cost for GST	137.25

GST - 18%	25.71
Landed cost in India	161.96
Retail Multiple	4
Selling Price	647.82
Difference	17%

The Financial Mistakes Continued

The goof-up in calculating the correct landed price of the imported shoe was just one instance of a comprehensive architecture of financial bungling.

My first error: the assumption that the maximum retail price (MRP as we know it) represented our cash inflow. For months, our realization implications had been based on this erroneous application of MRP; if we had to arrive at revenue projections, all we did was multiply the sticker price with the projected sales throughput. What we failed to recognize was something utterly simple: that the MRP comprised an 18 per cent GST component that we would need to collect on the government's behalf (over which we had no claim). Thereafter, our realizable price in the retail store would be the MRP less GST. For instance, if our MRP was 100 and GST 18 per cent, our realization would be Rs 85 (100/1.18). We always took 85 as 100, factoring in the GST credit. We also did not realize that we needed to consider discounts that we would need to offer.

It was weeks before we realized that there was a hole in our cash flow projections: we had forgotten to deduct the discount from the MRP. The result was that we would need to work that much harder to sell more and cover the deficit.

My second error: different GST rates applied in apparel based on your realized price and not MRP. I was not aware that whatever we realized from customers through apparel sale below Rs 1,000 would attract only 5 per cent GST; when we realized anything above, the applicable GST would shoot to 12 per cent. Because we calculated everything based on the MRP (and not realizable value or MRP less discount), the eyes were never trained to look at the critical numbers. Even if MRP was the same, say Rs 1,200, a 20 per cent discount would bring it down to Rs 960 and the GST would change.

My third error: the extensive discounts agreed by us as a team to various mom-and-pop distributors (20–50 per cent) without calculating our end realization. Because everyone was in a hurry to sell and generate cash, no one did this math before agreeing. As a result, there were times when our net realization was below our cost price. We sold at a loss. No one in the team did a discount sensitivity analysis that would tell us the quantum of loss at varying discount levels following commission deduction. By the time we finally began to correct this, the game had been lost.

My fourth error: no sharing of the ongoing P&L account with the rest of the organization. The stores had been signed without store managers being involved, so there was a reluctance to accept the targets that we were putting on them to get us to break even (quite like winning the toss on a batting wicket, putting the other team in to bat, then asking our bowlers to dismiss them for less than 100). I later discovered that if one had recruited the Head-Retail before we had signed our first store, he or she would have brought a new perspective on the right balance of store size, rent and projected sales throughput because of which the targets would have been 'owned'.

My fifth error: missing factoring the GST into the capital expenditure of our retail stores. Whenever I negotiated, it was always based on a cost per square feet multiplied by the total area. That gave me a fair idea of what we would need to pay the fabricator. However, when it was time to write the cheques, the fabricators explained, 'But the price we quoted to you was excluding GST. *Ab ispe aapko GST jodna padega* (You have to add GST to it).' Our store cap-ex bill of Rs 4 crore increased by Rs 72 lakh with the stroke of a pen.

My sixth error: the assumption that we would get our security deposits back from malls owners. When we decided to shut stores, the one clause that came back to bite us was the eighteen-month lock-in period (if we shut quicker, we would need to pay rent for all 18 months, adjusted with the security deposit). We could retrieve almost nothing by the time we ended.

My seventh error: the assumption that there would an attractive salvage value (25 per cent my estimate) of the Rs 4 crore fit-outs that had gone into our stores; we salvaged less than 1 per cent.

		BOTE*	Excel
Cost	A	400	425
Multiple		3.5	
MRP		1400	1400
Less: Discount		0%	30%
Realized MRP	B	1400	980
GST	C	12%	5%
GST Rs		150	46.67
MRP less GST	D	1250.00	933.00
Realized Multiple (gain)		3.13	2.2
Margin		68.05%	54.55%
* Back of the envelope			

A: Our landed cost was higher than anticipated from BOTE because we didn't factor freight, insurance and other costs like insurance.

B: We estimated that we would sell a majority of our inventory at full price (MRP); the question of discount was never brought into BOTE calculations.

C: GST rate changed with realized MRP; we didn't factor this.

D and E. Our margins (or multiple-to-cost) reduced by 50 per cent, affecting cash flows into D:FY.

26

The Not-So Discerning Customer

Sona ya peetal?

Diwali 2018.

T his is what we banked on. That time of the year when consumer spending in India peaks and people buy not just for the festival or season but for the year.

D:FY was prepared with a complement of seventeen stores in seven cities. Plus, online on Amazon.in.

Our stores were at the right place, at the right time, inside the sports zone of malls. Two retail outlets of more than 2,500 sq. ft were of an international standard. Our front-store executives were lively, product-informed and engaging. There was a treadmill in each store where one could try the feel of our shoes. In addition to shoes and apparel, we stocked accessories and caps. The aspiration of being global and yet Indian was beginning to emerge.

The consumer would walk into our store, look around, try our product, size up the large Hardik Pandya visuals, click a selfie ... and walk out with the apologetically whispered *'Thodi der me aata hoon.'* (I will come in a bit.)

Something deterred them from buying.

Interestingly, our apparel stock moved; the shoes did not. We needed a course-correction.

I showed the product to marathoning friends; they said 'Prashant, nothing wrong with the product, looks and feels absolutely great.'

I showed to our buying agent in Hong Kong (who was sourcing for Myntra and Wildcraft in India). He said, 'Excellent shoe, no question.' We critically assessed the product. Did not find any challenges. They were indeed good-looking. The worn comfort was great. We could not fault the product.

And yet, when we got to the consumer – the person who comes to shop with his or her family, where the purchase decision is influenced partly by the younger generation who has constantly been on Instagram or Facebook, who has been impressed by the shoes worn by the neighbour or his wife, who balances the monthly household budget, the verdict would surprisingly be 'Expensive.'

Expensive at Rs 3,000? Come on.

We were missing something.

Underestimating

At an MRP of Rs 3,000, we should have been selling around 250 shoes per day during the Diwali season 2018.

We were selling no more than fifty pairs per day.

We began to decode why.

Why 1: We felt we knew who our consumer was. People like us, simple. Every product and price decision were taken keeping a person like 'me' as the prospective consumer. As it turned out, the profile of people walking in to buy our products was completely different. He or she was not a well-to-do professional from Juhu (a posh neighbourhood in Mumbai) now getting serious about fitness; it was a profile completely opposite; it was someone at the mid-level corporate level seeking a sporty shoe and not a sports shoe; someone who would think a number of times before spending Rs 3,000 on a shoe with an unfamiliar brand name.

Why 2: The Indian consumer was still evolving. Absolute price mattered more than relative pricing or value. They were price-seekers, not value-seekers. The technology, the look, the aspiration and the experience mattered only if the product was available at their expected price and had a discount label attached. Else, it did not. When it came to sporty shoes, Rs 3,000 was not 'value'. The customer never cared for the mechanics that had gone into this Rs 3,000 shoe that would make it more functional and durable than a Nike or Adidas at Rs 5,000. The customer didn't care. It was always a glance at the price tag that made him/her raise an eyebrow and leave. In short, we misread our customer. It reminded me of a quote by the legendary investor Warren Buffett: *The street knows the price of everything and the value of nothing.*

Why 3: We underestimated the power of brands like Nike, Adidas, Reebok, Asics and Puma. These were no longer just brands; they had become cults. Wearing them was not about functionality; it was a statement that one had arrived. The result was that an end-of-season Nike, Adidas or Puma at Rs 4,000 (even when they had been fabricated in India) appeared more compellingly 'valued' than a D:FY at Rs 3,000. The challenge then was not in our product; it was the way a consumer perceived us. To them, we were a new, untested, unknown *Indian* brand. In sports shoes, they preferred Nike (sponsors of the Indian cricket team), Adidas (Sachin Tendulkar was its brand ambassador for over ten years) and Puma (Virat Kohli was its brand ambassador besides Usain Bolt). Why spend Rs 3,000 on D:FY when you can get the swoosh or the three stripes for a similar price?

By now the confidence had begun to wear thin; we had begun to hope instead.

The conversations of the past had begun to come back in snatches. Kishore Biyani had encapsulated the sports shoe category as 'difficult' with this explanation: 'When you compete as a start-up with the Nikes of the world, it is not just their product and price that you are competing with; you are competing with what that word "Nike" means to the consumer. And the interpretation of that word in the mind of the prospect is something that one has no way to influence.'

What Kishore Biyani was trying to explain was that even when you price comparably against a Nike, you have an icicle's chance in hell; when you price below Nike, you don't know at what price a consumer's disinterest can turn into a buying decision; when you price significantly below Nike, you have by then reduced yourself to a *sasta* (cheap) player with little chance of transforming into the next big Indian dream.

And yet. One was still not willing to give up. That lingering optimism was that Skechers had challenged Nike, Adidas, and Puma in India – the brand had started from scratch, focused on the walking category with easy-to-slip-into sporty shoes, connected with the masses and carved out a slice. I kept telling myself that all we had to do was to convince just 30,000 people to try D:FY, and once they did, they would know what we had built. The word of mouth would circulate.

I kept going back to ANTA. ANTA in China had encountered similar brand headwinds and emerged successful. So it could be done, and perhaps it was only a matter of time before we would address these glitches and be on our way. My mistake was to equate the Indian customer with the Chinese customer. China has always prided on wearing Chinese. Indians prided on wearing 'imported'.

Finally, one kept coming back to the lowest common denominator. If we had to sell 30,000 shoes across seventeen stores in seven cities (and Amazon) that would be seven pairs per day per store.

Each time I thought of that number, I felt no different from how the great Tendulkar had once dissected a 350 chase in a one-day match with the words: 'Hit one four, one two and a single in one over and after forty overs we will be 280, leaving us seventy to get in the last ten. How difficult is that?'

27

The Slip

Socha kuch, paaya kuch

Subsequent to our launch, we were expecting a certain minimum sales volume every week from the offline and online. It did not happen. At first, we did not seek to reconcile to the fact that the consumer was saying something. That either the product or price was the problem. While we were decoding this at the level of the offline, the constant message we got was that we needed visibility of the brand offline since consumers did not know the brand D:FY. We thought that once our Diwali campaign took off, our offline issue would be resolved.

We went to Amazon offices to get a grip on the volume offtake.

The Amazon team presented us some data. Our products were not selling well. I was taken aback. They also said it was early days and spoke of new brands launched at the same time as ours on Prime Day also doing similar volumes. We kept pushing for reasons. They cited several, based on their aggregated findings.

One, our product description was all over the place. What we thought was intelligent was proving to be not. For instance, we had four SKUs that we called 'multi-sport' shoes since this is how we had showcased them at our retail stores. However, no customer comes to Amazon.in and searches for multisport shoes. They were more likely to type 'sports shoes' or 'running shoes' or even 'walking shoes'. And because of this reason D:FY never showed up higher in the hierarchy of searches on Amazon. in. It was only visible to customers who went to 'exclusive brand launches'. On Amazon.in, content was king. The first line of product description needed words that Amazon's search engine and AI could pick up. To change that was another ball game. We did so, but not successfully. I realized that to succeed on Amazon.in one needed a certain direct-to-consumer mindset with a deep technology understanding. D:FY was built as a direct-to-consumer brand for offline customers trying to market on the online format. Fundamental mismatch.

Two, data showed, with advertising spends directly on Amazon.in platform, customers came and clicked on D:FY too, but then dropped off. Our click to revenue conversion was low. And this surprised us all. We thought we had a kickass product with all built-in features at attractive price. But that's not what customer thought. Much later I reconciled to how wrong we were. When I was researching and went to anta.cn, everything was around the 'look' of the product and 'price'. That's what attracted me. Perhaps the same with Indian shoppers on Amazon. We did not shoot the products separately to make them look sexy on the site. They were normal product shoot. Product needed to be shot like a model. Then the description needed to glamorize them. And then the price. In our initial days when traffic was high on D:FY on Amazon, we tried to sell at full price, no discount. The customer walked away. She was telling us, why would I come to shop on Amazon.in without any discount? Online thrived on 'perceived' value. The discount percentage was the most important decision driver. We did not get that right. We corrected that, but by then it was a bit late in the day. At the time of writing this book, D:FY was available on Amazon.in at a 65 per cent discount! If we had even agreed on 30–40 per cent discount at that time, the story could well have been different.

Three, to drive volumes on Amazon.in, the marketing competence required was needed to be different. This kind of marketing is called 'performance marketing'. The marketing focus is on making the customer click. It's about seduction. It's about playing on greed. We could never engage with a digital marketing team that understood this. Everyone claimed that they knew exactly how digital marketing worked. The reality is that we switched three digital marketing agencies. We just could not stand out. We needed the agility and intellect to decode why more customers were clicking a particular creative, and then use that insight to build more such creatives. Our problem was that we never gave Amazon.in the importance we should have. It was always the mistress for us, never the wife.

Four, online reputation management is critical. If you are a new brand you want other customers to become your brand ambassadors. Five-star reviews graduate your brand on the hierarchical search ladder. Better and more reviews make the next customer feel comfortable about buying a new brand. One needed to offer the right incentives to customers to fill reviews. We did not have a strategy and neither did any agency tell us that we needed one.

Five, at Amazon.in we had one more challenge. There existed a Chinese wall between Amazon.in and Cloudtail. Reviews, data on the number of customer visits, time spent, who dropped off in the first few seconds was the domain of Amazon. What sold and at what price was the domain of Cloudtail. And we could not decipher whom to listen to. Cloudtail would suggest performance marketing and intelligent discounting. For performance marketing we had to rely on Amazon. It was a kind of merry-go-round. What I realized later was that to succeed on Amazon, we needed performance marketing (to drive traffic) and discounts (for conversion) as a strategic tool to sell more. Why were we so concerned? Cloudtail had bought from us. The agreement said that if they did not sell, then they could return the inventory and get it replaced with next season's stock. This meant some of next season's inventory for which we paid (cash outflow) would not be purchased but replaced (no cash inflow). We needed Cloudtail to buy more from us in the second season, not merely seek replacements.

Six, because Amazon proved process-led and data-led, it could never suggest something out of the box. They always suggested what had worked for other brands. Besides, while we were engaged with Amazon, the team kept changing. The Bengali lady who had reached out to me to close the deal left for a food-tech company. The Cloudtail purchase person was made in-charge of electronics. The marketing person got busy with another campaign. Each time we started from scratch. The passion with which Amazon pitched around the partnership concept waned. That's when I realized that at Amazon one was always dealing with process and data, never people.

In the end D:FY never gave online the respect that format deserved. One needed to invest time in being able to understand nuances like the importance of product description, brand page, reviews and discount. A big mistake in hindsight was that of exclusivity. If I could time-travel, I would not have given Amazon exclusivity. If we had Amazon, Myntra, Flipkart, Jabong, TataCliq, Ajio, Snapdeal, Fynd selling for us, we would not only have sold more, but the data from all of them could have been profitably used. Who knows, despite the closure of our offline channel, D:FY may still have been relevant online and survived.

28

The Wall of Worry

Kuch toh gadbad hai

November 2018.

After three months in business, it was official. There was something seriously wrong within.

Rs 23 crore had been invested in the business. My net worth had eroded more than 60 per cent. What had taken 23 years to aggregate was gone in 23 months.

The problem was not that we were losing but that *we didn't know why*.

The promotional campaign had bombed. Our shoes were not selling. The rents and overheads were draining cash flows. What was going out was higher than what was coming in. The promoters were approaching their investment limit. Our warehouses were stocked. There was an imminent need to place Rs 10 crore of fresh orders from China for the new season (with 25 per cent advance) if we sought to retain merchandise freshness at the start of the second season.

The first manifestation of this troubled business state was sleep. I would wake up at 3 a.m. to stare at the ceiling for hours. I would replay the office events in the mind. I would keep simulating 'What if we had …' options.

On the mornings that followed, my Etna would erupt and spew ash on calls with Rajiv.

He would listen, agree, but remain unruffled. 'It is too early in the day to ascertain where and how we are going wrong,' he would sagely pronounce. 'We never sold as much when Puma was as small as we are today,' he would console me.

After some such one-sided conversations, I said *'Bahut hua!'* (Enough!)

I called an urgent meeting of important stakeholders (Rajiv's father, Rajiv, Ketan, Samir and I) to take stock.

We needed to spell out the truth.

Rajiv's father and I travelled to Bengaluru for the meeting.

Like a Feather in the Wind

I felt a distinct chill as I emerged from the Kempe Gowda International Airport in Bengaluru. Bengaluru is generally a cool city, but the winter had set in well in December 2018.

The chill was not just in the air, but also in my mood.

Winter is coming, I told myself while sipping Hatti Kappi and waiting for our ride.

The ride to our Bengaluru office in Indiranagar was largely quiet. Rajiv's father and I shared general gossip on the Indian stock markets (he is a stockbroker while I obsessed about equities). We beat the Bengaluru traffic since we had taken an early flight to get quicker to our office.

Indiranagar, where our office was located, was empty. The location marks the heart of Bengaluru's high-street shopping. As I alighted, I could see the flagship Chumbak store adjacent to us. Rubbing shoulders with our office was the ubiquitous Café Coffee Day (CCD). Just ahead was Puma's corporate building and store. If one walked around in a 2-km radius one could access almost every retail brand launched in India. Giving them company were several restaurants, coffee shops and bars.

Our office-cum-retail store was on the first floor. Below was a large Nature's Basket retail outlet that attracted affluent customers. The CCD next to us attracted millennials. Our retail store faced the main road where we had commissioned a large D:FY sign with Hardik Pandya wearing D:FY from head to toe. The D:FY signage lit up strikingly at night.

Our Bengaluru office was 1,700 square feet with a retail store of 800 square feet. We had designed the office tastefully. When we had rented the office, we knew it was big. I had seen how Future Group had invested in infrastructure ahead of growth. When we took the office, our plan was exactly that. We would keep growing without needing to relocate.

On that day in December 2018, I had 'invited' senior stakeholders. After months, all of us were together in person.

I commenced the meeting by lobbing a grenade. 'We should shut shop.'

These four words made those in attendance stiffen.

At D:FY, this was more than a social engagement. This was a call to arms.

I continued: 'Since we started, we have virtually exhausted over Rs 20 crore and are now required to invest a further Rs 10 crore for the business to survive another year.

'We have been retailing less than six months and are almost bankrupt.

'We do not know our consumer.

'We have a product that is not selling – either in our stores or on Amazon – even at a bloody discount.

'Our marketing campaign has not raised an eyebrow.

'Our recruitment has been completely wrong.

'Our supply chain has goofed up big time —'

Rajiv interrupted to present his take.

'Not many brands manage to launch seventeen stores in under three months.

'We have sales exclusivity with Amazon. They bought and paid Rs 5 crore. If they didn't believe, would they have done so?

'Our marketing campaign has just ended. The end-of-season sale is now starting and that's where volumes will happen. There is always a lag.

'Show me another start-up with Hardik Pandya, Anil Kumble and Farhan Akhtar as brand ambassadors.

'Brooks and New Era are actually doing well.

'We have just started the distribution business and people have shown interest.

'You need to be patient …'

'Patient? So that we could lose even more money?' I countered.

How many times had he visited the retail stores under construction? How many times had he spent quality time with frontline sales staff inside the stores?

Rajiv fought back. By his visiting the stores, consumers wouldn't buy more. Our retail head was in touch with what was happening inside the stores on a day-to-day basis. He was conducting daily reviews with Sudhakar, our principal merchandizer.

We were not seeing different things. We were seeing things differently.

When we dissolved for lunch, the general drift was that I had been excessively punishing (possibly) with my tone and temper. The team now rallied to defend D:FY. This was a new business. There was something called 'settling time'. Things were not as bad as I was making them out to be. Maybe we were ahead of our time. The tide would soon turn.

To balance the course of the meeting, we considered firefighting as well. Rajiv volunteered to broad-base the online business beyond Amazon. We selected to move Samir from Bengaluru to Mumbai. We agreed that with 40 per cent unsold inventory at the end of the first season (best case), we needed to sell, sell and sell more. We drew out a sales plan. We would broaden our coverage from retail and online to add distribution to mom and pop sports stores across the country. We would market products to pan-India distributors.

This is how the projected numbers began to look: If we generated Rs 8 crore from proprietary retail stores, Rs 9 crore from the distribution network and around Rs 12 crore from Amazon in the next 12 months, we could still save the company. Our challenge was not the speed of business but cash flows. We had grown too fast. And with revenues not catching up, the cash flow was pinching us more than the scale of business.

We needed more cash to sustain the ship. And as promoters, we had put almost all we had.

'Money is the least of our problems ,' I told myself.

But there was hope, or so we thought.

At Rs 30 crore revenue we could (when priced between 2 and 3x) get a Rs 75–Rs 90 crore valuation. This valuation could interest investors, strengthen cash flows and provide us the oxygen to make it to the second season. And gradually that vicious cycle could transform into a virtuous circle.

The air cleared.

It always does when you pepper a conversation with words like 'private equity' and 'valuation'. Suddenly the business appears to be larger (even if it is losing Rs 70 lakh a month on a turnover of Rs 1.25 crore). It was an old trick: shifting the focus from 'what was' to 'what could be'; shifting the attention from a large loss to an exciting valuation.

I turned to Utpal Sheth. Utpal touched the pulse: 'You need to correct your financial structure. There is too much of personal net worth in it. Raise at least Rs 20 crore. That will give you cash flow, breathing room and time to evolve. It will also introduce you to a business-neutral mind (investor) who will set the priorities right, keeping in mind shareholder value creation as the overall goal.'

29

Hope

Ummeed pe duniya qaayam hai

When we had invested Rs 2 crore in our maiden promotional campaign in November 2018, we had had two things going for us: seventeen pan-India retail stores and a campaign timed with the festive season that extended from Diwali into Christmas coupled with a time when most people move outdoors for increased physical activity (onset of winter).

Our estimate was that by the end of End-Of-The-Season-Sale (EOSS) in January 2019, we would have liquidated around Rs 7 crore of merchandise, averaging around Rs 3.5 crore a month (Rs 1.7 crore from our proprietary stores, Rs 0.5 crore from online sales and Rs 0.8 crore from a distribution network).

When we finished at a third of it – around Rs 1 crore a month – the disappointment was not just with the quantum: it was that the sales proceeds were around the identical level we had been averaging *before* our campaign and *before* the festive season.

This is the moment when entrepreneurs lose hope; we continued to believe that the products were compelling. Our conversion rate was still a good ~27 per cent. Every third person who came bought. The challenge lay elsewhere: we needed to get more people into our stores and for that we needed to keep spending on advertising and marketing. We needed to pour more cash into the company. The bottom line: We needed to get an external investor.

In the preceding months, we had often been speaking with potential investors since they had liked what we were executing. Because we were busy with execution, we had not prospected for capital. However, some of the downsides that investors did communicate about our business were that we were doing too many things at the same time; we were a high-capital-intensive business (which Utpal Sheth had also indicated); we were sitting at a high-stakes table; our valuation expectations were high; we had possibly bitten off more strategically than we could chew operationally.

This feedback got me thinking. In most cases, external investors would complain of strategic and execution challenges; here we had rolled out stores at possibly the fastest speed within the business, engaged Amazon, collaborated with Brooks and New Era, engaged marquee brand ambassadors, generated a healthy conversation rate, got a business up and running in no time, we had done all this with our own capital and they were saying we were doing too much too fast. Bloody hell.

We didn't just need a financial investor; we needed a strategic investor. I began to entertain a wild idea: Why not Kishore Biyani himself? He could refine our marketing direction. He could get us footprint in Central and Brand Factory. He could enhance our valuation with his mere association. He would provide us access to the rich knowledge bandwidth of Future Group.

I went ahead and pitched.

I kept it high-level: we had three brands, D:FY, Brooks and New Era; we had retail, online and mom-and-pop distribution; we had Hardik Pandya and Farhan Akhtar as brand ambassadors; we understood sports footwear and had designs for two more seasons ready including technological tie-up with BASF and Bloom; we had invested Rs 25 crore of our personal capital; there was no debt on our books.

We were weak in just one area: getting customers into our stores (marketing). This is where he excelled. We needed to raise Rs 25 crore of external capital. Rather than raise from any financial investor, why not bring in Future Group as a strategic one.

Here came the surprise. Kishore Biyani agreed.

He added a disclaimer: 'I won't put in the whole Rs 25 crore that you need, but I can put in around Rs 5–7 crore subject to my Board's approval and due diligence. The rest you raise from the others, which should not be difficult once Future Group's name has been associated with D:FY.'

Deal.

The various arms started moving quicker thereafter. One prominent Family Office agreed to put down Rs 2–3 crore. Friends and associates committed Rs 5 crore.

Then something even more interesting happened.

Nikhil Vora and Sixth Sense

I had known Nikhil Vora (founder of Sixth Sense, a hugely successful investor in brand-led companies and arguably India's most respected consumer analyst-turned-investor in the consumer space) for long. Nikhil's focus was to back brands and new-age entrepreneurs that were challenging behemoths.

I sounded him about D:FY. He sounded interested; given the size of his fund, he needed to invest at least Rs 30 crore, he said. The word trickled to a prominent Kolkata conglomerate and it came in with an appetite for Rs 10 crore. A conversation through Ritesh Sidhwani (Excel Entertainment) led us to another listed retailer (quite like Future Group) who moved the conversation from launching D:FY as shop-in-shop in their stores to becoming an equity partner.

We may have been bleeding money, but to investors like Future Group and others there was value in what we had achieved.

We had got to a point where we were almost beginning to ration fresh equity.

And to think that just a few weeks before, I had suggested that we should close down.

30

The Calm before the Storm

Shanti … toofan se pehle ki

January 2019.

D:FY may not have broken even but it had built a fund-raising visibility of around Rs 45 crore.

What was critical was the value that prospective investors were intending to put on our company. If they priced us too low, we would have sold a large quantum of shares at a low price. While this would have increased the equity size of the company, it would have moderated the stake of the promoters in the company. The lower our skin in the game, the more distant would have been our dream to build our personal fortunes.

The objective then was to package a story well enough with all the positives we had achieved to be able to get a pre-money valuation of Rs 75 crore. However, Sixth Sense offered a pre-money valuation of Rs 55 crore. If we raised Rs 40–45 crore, the holding of the promoters (Rajiv and I) would have been diluted by 45 per cent, and my 50 per cent stake in the company would have declined to 27.5 per cent following the first dilution, leaving us with low equity ammunition should we have needed to dilute a second time.

We would need to raise further capital in the next twenty-four months if we wished to keep growing. This would have meant that we as promoters would have ended up working for our investors. They would become majority owners and we would be reduced to a minority.

I had a brainwave. If indeed we had to work for an investor group, why not work for Future Group with a minority stake? I presented this approach to Kishore Biyani. He liked the idea. Since Future Group owned a sports brand (Spunk) that catered to a customer segment a notch below D:FY's price range, he suggested: we converge Future Group's Spunk brand and D:FY's brands (D:FY and Brooks) to create a consolidated portfolio that would appeal to a wide cross-section of customers.

This is where it got interesting: The FG brand that we wanted merged already had over Rs 350 crore in revenues (largely from sports apparel and modest sports footwear revenues). Kishore Biyani suggested that the FG team would continue to drive apparel revenues while we would be required to drive the footwear business; the combined business would be required to mobilize its own resources to grow the business without recourse to the FG balance sheet. He would allow us to lead the combined entity.

There comes a moment in one's life when the gloom of the years parts in one magical moment and one can feel the adrenalin in one's knees. This was it.

The coming of the brands would result in a wider range (Brooks at the apex, D:FY in the middle and Spunk addressing mass consumers); the company that our business would be transferred to would be profitable from day one; we would get the entire distribution pipeline of FG; we would get access to FG's marketing spring board. Even though we would be reduced to minority ownership, the valuation of our minority stake would be higher than the current value of our majority stake since the pie would have increased manifold.

I told myself: *Dekhna (see), capital will chase us from now onwards.*

The FG deal came with riders. Rider 1: The merger needed to pass a strict compliance filter. Rider 2: FG's Board would need to approve the transaction. Rider 3: We would need to manage our financials until FG came in. Rider 4: Even as FG was engaged in fund-raising of its own, we drew out a timeline within which the transaction could proceed – Kishore Biyani needed to close this by March 2019.

The only point that concerned Rajiv and I: How much stake will we eventually own in the combined entity? I didn't discuss this with Kishore Biyani. *'Dekha jaayega'* (we will see), I said. We had a certain idea in mind. Based on my investing experience, my sense was that if the combined entity generated revenues of Rs 350–400 crore and was profitable (indicative EBIDTA of 9–10 per cent), then the combined business should have been valued at Rs 600 crore based on a conservative 1.5–2x price-to-revenue multiple. Given a Rs 55 crore valuation for D:FY, we reckoned that we would get a 10 per cent stake in the combined entity. In *rokda* (cash) terms, it meant that we had invested Rs 25 crore, and within 24 months, it would have grown to Rs 55 crore.

I bowed to the Great Biyani. Well, almost.

The next day, we called the financial investors whom we had been prospecting. We explained we had decided to go to bed with FG. Most told us that what we had done was right; going with FG was the best for our business. To soften their disappointment, we welcomed them to participate in the fund-raising for the combined entity. They said they would evaluate once the businesses had merged.

What remained was to complete the FG due diligence. FG audited every piece of inventory on our books. No discrepancy was found. We now needed to get our act going and correct our mistakes. We focused on moderating our FOB cost of product and move the manufacturing to India. We worked on a new line of footwear that was 'sneaker-like' but not sporty. We engaged with designers from Spain. We had got a second chance.

If only we knew what was coming.

Many a Slip between the Cup and the Lip

We needed to pay our Chinese suppliers for the shoes we would be ordering for the second season. We had placed the order for limited quantities. We looked to FG to help us with bridge funding.

Future Group said it would not be able to loan us. Since we were confident that the deal with FG would go through, we took a 90-day bill discounting facility of Rs 1.6 crore for the first time. We were now in debt, with our equity virtually eroded.

We were banking on the deal with FG. We took one more bet. The merger got deferred to the first quarter of 2019–20 from March 2019. It stretched us since we were losing Rs 1 crore a month. We decided to stay in the game with our last hope.

Then we were told that there could be a delay of another three months. We could disengage from the agreement, shut the business or invest additionally for three months to keep the conversation alive. But we needed to bridge the funding gap since we were still losing money every month due to our retail business.

In the next three months, we infused Rs 5 crore into D:FY by scrounging for whatever cash one could raise. Personally, I mortgaged my house, borrowing Rs 3 crore against it.

Meanwhile, the merger kept getting delayed. Rajiv, who had until then been counselling patience, snapped. 'I can't invest more,' he stated. We had two choices – wait or wilt. I kept going back to FG. The standard response: 'We are certainly interested but we need time.'

Here we were haemorrhaging, and there was no urgency from the prospective partner. I told FG where one stood. The only way to survive was to take our crown jewel – retail business – out of play. FG nodded. They said anyways they had enough retail so if shutting down helped us they were backing us on the move. Immediately shut the bleeding, they said.

I conferred with Rajiv on the need to wait, shut our retail stores, plug the drain and wait for the day when FG would be ready to walk with us down the aisle to the altar.

He agreed.

31

Death

Ram naam satya hai

August 2019.

One year after we had done everything right and inaugurated our maiden retail store in Phoenix Marketcity (Kurla), with Kishore Biyani, Anil Kumble, Farhan Akhtar and Ritesh Sidhwani, we called it quits on the retail front.

We had invested Rs 8.5 crore in security deposits and furniture and fixtures. When we negotiated with our vendors to return the retail fixtures, lighting and air-conditioners, the words they used were *'scrap value mein bikega'* (you will get scrap value). This meant that we would not be paid for the functional value of the asset; we would be paid by weight (*'Kilo ke bhaav se'* to use the vernacular). The lighting would be of no use, we were told, as no one would buy pre-used. The AC units would generate some salvage value, but the mall contract stipulated that when we returned the store, they required it in the same condition it had been given (read 'bare shell'). That meant that we would have to undo everything ... at an additional cost. This meant that to undo our precious cap-ex we would have to spend addition cap-ex. What we recovered from Rs 4 crore of fittings could be counted in the small lakhs. This 'conspiracy' of the universe affected my family life, relationships, conversations and fitness (a scenario quite like when my closest friend passed away at thirty-seven in February 2014).

When we were winding down, I was sure to recover the security deposits paid on mall space occupation. They were, after all, a 'deposit' and hence secured. When we reached out, they said, 'You owe us, friend; we don't.' They indexed down to our agreement which stipulated a mandatory lock-in period of eighteen months. Since we were closing 6–9 months short, they were entitled to deduct rent for the balance period from our rent payable for the balance lock-in period was higher than our deposit. The mall developers were now no longer talking their saccharine marketing language; they said that they would not allow us to retrieve stock from our stores until we had cleared their account (we settled amicably with Phoenix Mills through a friendly intermediary). We may have got nothing back from them, but we settled with no dues to them. The Rahejas were considerate and returned a small amount. Other developers accommodated; one initiated legal action.

The negotiation with mall owners, low sales, and a waiting game for FG to get into bed with us cumulatively did one thing. Drained energy.

Then came the momentous call with Rajiv. I entered the Mumbai office-cum-store at Laxmi Industrial Estate, in Andheri West, at 9.30 a.m. As I was preparing my to-do list, I called

Rajiv. Nothing serious but trivial. He too was facing the heat (though I wanted to believe that I was enduring far more, and in retrospect I must concede that perhaps he never showed it more than I did).

He asked if there was any FG update. Simple question. I took it as a veiled accusation. He was seeking functional information. I was looking for a joust. Rather than explain that I too was frustrated with the delay, which would have been the usual thing to do, I launched my first punch. I counter-enquired on details about his share of the impending fund infusion, sales details of specific retail store closures and discussions with mall owners on security deposit refunds. How dare he ask me about FG when his plate was not clean?

My questions may have been civil; my tone was not. Gradually, as the conversation progressed, the punches began to be directed at the belt – and even lower. The conversation that had commenced with the civil was now insulting. The pitch had increased. I was trading charges. I was attacking on all fronts.

Rajiv responded with calm. 'Prashant,' he said, 'This is not working out for me. I don't wish to continue. Even if the FG deal comes through, I don't wish to be a part of this any longer. I will start searching for a professional job right away.'

I didn't think I had heard right. When it sank in, my knees quivered. I countered aggressively that this was not fair. Rajiv remained Rajiv. Firm. Calm. Unchanging.

I was alone. Finally.

I responded aggressively that even his fortune was at stake and that this was not the way he could shrug his responsibility off. He said he had decided. Irrevocably.

We eventually agreed on a few aspects that required him to shoulder some responsibility (operationally and financially) after which Rajiv ended his formal innings at D:FY. I too gave up thereafter. The fight had gone out of me. I gave myself time till September 2019, following which if the FG deal had not transpired, I decided I would move on as well. I kept turning to FG as a last resort. From a time when I would get an instant WhatsApp reply from Kishore Biyani, I had moved down in his priority list where I would not get a reply even after seven messages. One day I asked FG's CFO for direction. He was concerned. 'Even though the probability of the deal happening remains intact, the timing is undecided. We have a lot happening at our end. If I were you, I would look elsewhere.'

The Last Hope

The loss was staggering.

The business had consumed Rs 30 crore including what had been borrowed on bill discounting (Rs 1.6 crore).

Almost everything I had earned had been frittered.

As I awaited the next turn in my destiny, I turned to Utpal Sheth for two reasons. To confess that his faith in me and our business had been unfounded; to explore the possibility of finding a white knight investor for D:FY who would resurrect the ship.

Utpal's gut feel was that Future Group would come around since Kishore Biyani had not formally turned the proposal down. Despite this last hope, Utpal insisted on something more fundamental: a stop-loss (to limit loss or gain in a trade) after which I could write off all losses and move on. He did not feel that a white knight would be interested in putting money into the business since we had closed our retail stores and were now reduced to a distribution business. I countered: a distribution business is exactly what he was suggesting in the first place and now we were actually one; besides, it was not just a distribution business as we possessed inventory (MRP value of Rs 20 crore), three exclusive brands (D:FY, Brooks and New Era); the second season's merchandise was far more evolved than the first; the technology in our shoes would upgrade in season three with the infusion of BASF and Bloom; we had excellent brand ambassadors in Hardik Pandya and Farhan Akhtar; our mistakes would now become our learnings.

We possessed a foundation; all we needed was growth capital.

Utpal felt there was a case in my counter-argument. He said, 'Let us go meet Rafique Malik (owner of Metro shoes where Rakesh Jhunjhunwala is presently an investor and Utpal sits on its Board).'

We had met Rafique Malik on an earlier occasion when we were trying to convince him to distribute our products through his Metro and Moji chain of stores. Rafique Malik had come across as a man of integrity who had applauded our thought leadership, passion and products. However, that discussion had gone nowhere; Metro did not feel comfortable showcasing a new brand.

But now things were a bit different. We possessed a year of experience. We had identified local sourcing. We had worked on our pricing. Utpal debriefed Rafique Malik that we needed a strategic partner. Rafique Malik accorded me the respect of an entrepreneur and spoke with dignity. He agreed that we needed to moderate our price to a sweet spot of Rs 2,000 and still deliver a 65 per cent gross margin; he agreed with our decision to make India a sourcing base. Where he had second thoughts was that even as his non-formal category was growing faster than his formal wear (Metro being respected for formality), his customers preferred buying established brands. Besides, Metro focused on faster inventory turns, an area where the company had unfavourable experiences with relatively untried brands like ours. I pitched that D:FY would be like Metro's private label (own brand) and since Metro had several private formal labels in its portfolio, ours could help Metro extend its line to address the sneakers trend. I emphasized that besides inventory, new design, local sourcing and brand ambassadors, Metro would benefit from our team experience, an advantage that few Indian labels possessed. We said we would be open to yielding management control with an equity swap.

I walked to the white board and listed:

- Brand with Hardik Pandya (locked in for five years), Farhan Akhtar and Krunal Pandya
- Inventory at cost of ~Rs 6.5 crore *on hand*
- New season collection *ready*
- New sourcing *ready*
- New range of sneakers, designed in Spain, *ready*
- Entire team, including Rajiv and me, *ready to execute*.

Rafique Malik said he would revert. He did. He said 'no'.

Rajiv recommended we make a similar pitch to Reliance Brands, headed by his former Arvind colleague Darshan Mehta. He wrote to Darshan and set up a meeting. Rajiv and I went. Darshan and I connected (he had once headed the securities business for Sanjay Lalbhai and built Anagram Finance). The pitch to him was different. Reliance Brands had built a reputation for partnering global brands like Armani Exchange, Muji, Steve Madden, Diesel, GAS, G-Star RAW, Marks & Spencer and others. It had bought the entire luxury brand portfolio from the Indian partner for brands like Hugo Boss, Jimmy Choo, Salvatore Ferragamo, Tumi, Paul & Shark, etc. It had acquired Hamleys globally. However, Reliance Brands had nothing in the sports category. We pitched ourselves as a platform comprising D:FY, Brooks and New Era (the last two being global brands). He liked our pitch and called his team to meet us.

At Reliance Brands, the process came first. The team told us it would order some of our products first and test them. It sent us an Excel spreadsheet on our costs and margins structure from every channel, and inventory details. Being an investment banker and now an entrepreneur, I learnt a lot from that sheet. Based on perception, Reliance gave me the impression that it would buy anything it liked at any price; that sheet conveyed a different story that the company's God lay in the details, and based on that spreadsheet, it would never overpay.

The first good news: The Reliance team indicated that our products had passed their stringent test. It added that it would revert on the next few steps. We waited impatiently. Darshan reached out. Rajiv was in Bengaluru, so I went alone to meet him. In less than five minutes, Darshan said 'no' and took the next thirty minutes to explain why. He said he liked the Brooks and New Era brands. The problem with both was that Brooks was a performance running shoe and that Reliance Brands had previously partnered with Asics and Saucony. Brooks conflicted, and besides, he doubted Brooks' ability to ramp up in a price-sensitive long-distance running market (he was partially right; we had experienced that in Brooks as well). Runners liked to wear Brooks but only if the shoes were discounted. Besides, Darshan said, our Brooks agreement was for only five years, whereas Reliance Brands needed at least twenty years' exclusivity. When it came to New Era, Reliance Brands conceded that the brand was indeed an icon that it would have liked to include it in its portfolio but for the small size of India's caps market, the fact that headgear was not seen as a fashion accessory in India – most bought caps to protect from the sun – and even if successful, the size of New Era's business would still be a small decimal of Reliance Brands' overall income statement. And lastly, Darshan felt that D:FY did not fit into the Reliance Brands vision because we were engaged in concurrently building the brand and the product as opposed to the Reliance Brands commitment to sell, sell and sell without worrying about design and product development; as an extension, no brand could become a part of the Reliance Brands portfolio unless every store had broken even.

We moved on and pitched to Snapdeal, the erstwhile leader in the e-commerce space, before yielding to Flipkart and Amazon. Snapdeal was resurrecting itself, focusing on cash flows around the right business model. We met Snapdeal's founders and pitched D:FY as a brand that could become its private label, building their sports portfolio, sourcing locally and providing Hardik Pandya and Farhan Akhtar as brand ambassadors in addition to a Rs 20 crore MRP inventory. Sadly, Snapdeal had evolved into an only-platform model where different brands could market their products with Snapdeal building proprietary brands.

In fifteen days, we had been turned down three times.

It was time.

I had lost my father when I was seven in 1979.

The image of administering the last rites to a father came back to me in an altered form.

I was now being asked to administer the last rites to a metaphorical child. *My company.*

A number of people who read this are likely to question the analogy: by what stretch of imagination can one consider a non-living intangible creation to be a 'child'?

D:FY was a family member; I breathed D:FY; I lived D:FY. Now came the time to bury it.

I didn't have to. I could have extended its life by a few more months; the doctors could have tried the ventilator. But in the end, it would have been the delay of the inevitable.

With each passing say, the child would descend deeper into an irreversible coma. The dilemma: pull the plug and face reality or extend the misery in the hope of a recovery?

Reality versus hope. Reality prevailed.

It was time to pull D:FY off the ventilator and let go.

The last tip of the metal inched below the surface within thirty months of the time our liner had rolled off the shipyard and everyone touched their fingers to their lower lips and said, 'Wow! This will create history.'

My friend Devang Gandhi (former Test cricketer and national selector for Team India) was asked how he would have liked to be remembered when he retired.

'As someone who tried,' he had said.

Ditto.

Reflections

What could I have done differently?

'You make mistakes. Mistakes don't make you.'

Distance does not only lend enchantment to the view; it also enhances objectivity.

This realization came a few months after we had closed for business when I did a review of how we could have adapted in time to save the business and stayed in the game longer without necessarily breaking even but acquiring deeper insights to plug the cash drain before turning around.

Wisdom after the event is scarcely useful, except that in this case, it has made me a mellower person with a larger appetite for dissenting perspectives, wider risk understanding and larger openness to the suddenness of change outside one's control.

D:FY depleted me as a financial entity; on the other hand, it transformed me as a person for the better.

These are some of the things that I should have done differently.

1

Wealth creation should have been a by-product and not the core purpose.

As I grew older, little did I realize that the demons I had nursed through my childhood would begin to assert their independence. The result is that I did not just develop a desire to make more money (who doesn't?); it was the intensity of that obsession that had become the difference. There was a point when the value of my personal net worth had become the only score by which I was willing to measure my existence. I became the batsman who after getting to fifty now wanted to get to 200 (forget 100) and after getting to a double century wanted to get to 500.

I lost sight of why I was batting in the first place – for my team and for the pleasure of putting bat to ball. The sole purpose of why one was doing what one was doing was lost in the brat race: the evangelist in me was displaced by the capitalist. The original desire of creating a fitter India had been elbowed off-stage by the prospect of getting rich enough fast enough.

The word 'purpose' should have been defined and embraced. For instance, if someone had asked me whether I would have liked to have had 100 people at my funeral (the Stephen Covey yardstick of life impact appraisal) to be in awe of the personal wealth I had created or have 2,000 people regretting my passing away and in debt for the way I had transformed their lives, the answer would have been simple. The Rs 200 crore of personal wealth that I desired could have been a mission and goal; it could never have been the singular purpose of my existence (which it became).

A focus on creating a healthier and fitter idea could have kept me in business longer; and somewhere on that multi-year journey, our business would have grown to a point where my personal shareholding would have been worth Rs 200 crore. This lack of clarity on the difference between vision (cannot be achieved) and mission (roadmap) led to the downfall of my company and my net worth.

2

I participated in a bull market of arrogance.

I recognized the importance of harmony the more expensive way.

Look at it this way: I started my professional life with no confidence. I felt everyone was better (or at least better-placed) than I was. They would do better in life than I would; they would make more money than I would; they would be respected more by the world than I would.

What transpired was that following my first experience of academic success at twenty-three, there was a hockey stick turn in my confidence. Every stage of improvement, growth and promotion seeded a new idea: I was going to win. Each time I compared myself with others, I realized I was quicker and better. Each professional move and incremental risk I took turned out more successful.

The ultimate high transpired at FT, the company where I was employed, where even as it was passing through its most critical challenge, I experienced the biggest achievement of my career – promotion to MD and CEO. This was like a stock trebling even as the broad market was crashing. This validated my conviction: I was a non-cyclical stock in an unpredictable world.

It was not likely for someone with my credentials to turn defensive at that point. What would I have told myself? That I would remain CEO and MD for the rest of my life? That I would never make more money than I had at FT? Was I an astrologer to have imposed caution to myself? Since I had grown rapidly, it was only reasonable to assume that the momentum would sustain. I wasn't being recklessly optimistic in assuming this; anyone in my position would have made such an estimation of my prospects.

So, if I did select to graduate to the next level of respect, achievement and wealth, it was only logical. I was fortunate to have discovered a vehicle for this transformation: sneakers. I liked the subject. I was reasonably acquainted with users and I was lucky to have found a gateway in Alibaba.com and the Canton Fair. There was more to come: validation from whomever I spoke to about the quality of what I was intending to produce and market. Rajiv Mehta said 'great' and came in as partner. Anil Kumble said 'winner' and offered to come in as shareholder. How could one have become defensive from that point onwards?

However, the validation of all those I showed the sneakers to contributed to my undoing in an indirect way. They gave me confidence and validation; I could have transformed that feedback into a sense of confidence; I transformed it into a body of ego. I did not merely convince myself that the shoes would sell; I convinced myself that the shoes had 'already been sold' and that the proceeds were just lying in a corner for me to go and collect.

My ego was the size of the nation's debt. There were people who dissented politely – politely because they did not wish to discourage the entrepreneur in me – but the wine of my arrogance poured over their gentle apprehensions. The Father of Modern Indian Retail advised me to re-appraise my business model with words like *'Ek baar soch lo'* (Think once again), and I said to myself, 'What does he know?'

Sanjiv Agrawal (ex-MD, Skechers) asked me to visit more retail stores to understand reality and return with my observations for him and I to examine. I never went back to him again. ('Who wants to hear negative *bhaashan* [lecture]?')

Santosh Desai (Future Brands) said there was no shortage of imported sneakers available around Rs 3,000 and that a market did not quite exist. I dismissed his observation as bookish and academic.

Utpal Sheth (Rakesh Jhunjhunwala's partner) told me that the business model was high-risk and would trip at the first hiccup; I proceeded regardless.

I worked hard, did not compromise on the product and should have – by a conventional yardstick – succeeded. I failed because I refused to listen: when my questions did not conform to the answers I expected to hear, I shot the messenger.

I was a victim of the need for confirmation bias.

3

The high risk, high reward game got me.

Everyone champions the cause of risk-taking. What few champion is the cause of prudent risk-taking.

I couldn't see the risks in the business. (How difficult could it be to sell 34,000 pairs of shoes in six months in a country of 1.35 billion?) The result is I bet big.

In retrospect, I miscalculated on some fronts: I was surrounded with colleagues of a similar disposition; the D:FY ecosystem did not possess a single individual who possessed the intellect or courage to offer a contrary opinion. We were like a group of fund managers who not only believed in a bull market; we believed stocks would rise in every trading session.

Looking back, we should have reduced the bet in four places.

One, when Rajiv entered the partnership with his equity infusion, one should have retained the size of the bet and locked away his contribution into our reserves (we ended up betting with it).

Two, when Utpal Sheth cautioned against opening a number of D:FY stores and retail through partners like Central and Shoppers Stop, it should have been a good idea to grow the business while retaining our asset-lightness.

Three, when venture capitalists expressed an investment interest in D:FY, one should have pursued the subject. This would have moderated the promoter's risk in the venture; it would have tested my hypothesis of the market opportunity through some smaller lots of off-the-shelf shoes and apparel from China; it would have infused an independent perspective in our business model from the inside.

Four, one should have commenced the venture with a complement of online retail, departmental stores and a couple of D:FY exclusive stores (course-correcting all the time in line with consumer traction). The business would then have commenced with low risk and perhaps stayed that way even as the overall business got larger.

The reality, in cricket terminology, was that we did not know where our off stump was. The result is that we were bowled by an in-swinger.

4

We should have mobilized capital early on.

In my previous avatar as an investor, I asked entrepreneurs: 'If your story is so good, why don't you sell your property and put all your cash into the business?'

In my mind, the proposition was simple: if the business is good, bet your house on it; if not, exit. This was a binary approach: all or nothing, black or white, 0 or 1. There was no middle ground. Besides, if the promoter was not putting 100 per cent of his or her capital into the business, what moral right did he/she have to ask others to invest?

This represented my rationale for not diluting equity. However, what I did not consider was that venture capitalists and private equity investors exist for a larger reason than most care to appreciate: they do not just proffer cash to share the upside; they engage to share the risk as well (for which they are compensated when the business turns successful).

If I resisted the temptation to dilute our promoter stake through an infusion of venture capital, it was for two reasons. One, I selected to put my cash on the business before asking others. Two, I did not wish to invite others (and dilute our promoter stake) only to repent when the business became prosperous.

In retrospect, the induction of an external independent non-executive investor would have created the role for a neutral umpire and broad-based the funding pipeline.

The lesson as it turned out: promoters need skin in the game, but not the entire skin.

5

I did not know my customer.

One of the earliest lessons I learnt at Future Group: 'You are not your customer.'

This lesson I dismissed when I started D:FY. I assumed what worked for me would also work for my customers.

I felt the customer would be discerning enough to ignore the price and focus on value. I was comprehensively wrong.

I thought the consumer would buy into the concept of an Indian brand with pride. I was wrong.

I thought my running friends represented my consumers. I was wrong.

I thought my consumers would use my product when exercising. I was wrong.

Kishore Biyani was the first to flag this alert when he saw the way my advertisement had been designed by Grey Worldwide. He said: 'People in India don't wear Skechers and Nike while they are exercising. They wear these shoes because they are comfortable and easy on their knees.' He added that travelling Gujaratis, Marwaris and Punjabis loved wearing sneakers below their formal trousers when they travelled or to work. So, he asked me to remove the word 'sports' and just retain the words 'shoes' and 'apparel'.

When we launched our stores and online presence, I realized how I had miscalculated. The low consumer traction resulted in an inability to cover fixed costs. What I thought would be a virtuous cycle (excess of revenues over fixed costs) became a vicious cycle that pulled us deeper into the vortex.

6

I chose to build the brand ahead of the business.

For a consumer-interfacing product, brand building is an expensive proposition.

This is more so in a country like India, marked by a large land mass and the second most populous body of consumers.

At D:FY, our competition did not come in the form of mere products; it came in the form of the Nike Swoosh and Adidas' three stripes. We had no choice; we were compelled to create a brand from the day we went into business, which warranted the engagement of brand ambassadors and a presence in diverse media (print, out-of-home, digital, radio and TV).

The result was an expensive proposition that we approached the wrong way. We overspent on the building of the brand than the brand spend itself. The cost of ambassadors, agencies, shoot and retainers came to Rs 2.15 crore; the brand spend was only Rs 1.5 crore.

When our revenues did not match and drained our cash flows, we almost stopped our brand spending, which kick-started our vicious cycle.

Given the formidable strength of brands like Nike and Adidas, we should have built a business around known brands. We should have got an ANTA (Chinese brand) into India. We should have raised additional capital. We should have focused on one medium (digital) and deepened our investments in it.

As it turned out, we built a brand before we built a business; we invested our finite capital across media in one of the largest underpenetrated markets in the world.

Our voice was drowned out from day one.

7

I did not build the right team.

In building the D:FY team, I selected familiarity over competence.

What I gained in terms of integrity and commitment I lost on ideas and experience.

Later, when I tried the latter approach (competence), I lost out on trust.

In retrospect, I would have preferred competence over familiarity.

The other area where I made an error was that we built a top-heavy team that comprised individuals whom I considered friends and family. The result is that one struggled to segregate the personal from the professional.

One could have defined roles and responsibilities more precisely, which resulted in overlap, confusion and pain. If the strength of the chain is equivalent to its weakest link, then team selection was a big chink in our armour.

If one had focused more on team selection and responsibility identification, outcomes would have been different. Wherever we sought competence coupled with clarity of expectations and role definition, the outcomes were better.

But that was too little in too small a part of the company to make any impact. Sadly.

8

One in hand is better than two in the bush.

Should we have accepted the funding from financial investors like Nikhil Vora's Sixth Sense when it was available? Should I have taken the revised proposal about working for Kishore Biyani rather than take it to investors?

On the one hand, I would have been in complete control of my destiny had I diluted our ownership in favour of private investors even as driving the big idea would have been a challenge. On the other hand, Kishore Biyani's coming into the company would have helped D:FY merge with FG, giving us scale and visibility while linking our destiny to his.

I conceptually pushed for the latter because deep down I was not sure of D:FY's prospects even if we could have mobilized funds. Besides, the second option was easier with a limited downside.

What one had not factored in was that the deal with Future Group would not happen even after it had been conceptually cleared by the Big Man himself. The reality is that the worst case played out and I was compelled to mortgage my house to raise cash for the next net worth infusion into the business.

The delay claimed a casualty; Rajiv, my co-promoter, opted out of the business, and I surrendered.

I had one in my hand but went for the two in the bush and paid for it.

9

I did not celebrate my wins.

There is a natural tendency of the mind to ponder the negative over the positive.

The result is that we don't celebrate wins, small or big.

Whenever something positive transpired within the company, my immediate reaction would be *'Isme kya badi baat hai?'* (What's the big deal in this?)

I never gave myself an opportunity to feel good or be happy. What I overlooked was an important life lesson: success doesn't lead to happiness, but happiness leads to success.

At FT, I took big risks and was amply rewarded. When I left FT, I should have paused, celebrated and expressed gratitude. That precious sabbatical would have calmed. Instead, the reverse transpired: I did not see it as a win at all. I gritted, took fresh guard and subjected myself to an even larger target: more money. The crest of one achievement was planned to lead to another crest. There were to be no valleys in my existence.

It was like the coach forbidding the gold-medal-winning decathlete an ice cream after the Olympics was over.

10

If only I had controlled my temper ...

There is an interesting argument that the battle of Mahabharat may never have needed to be fought if the Pandavas had asked for their share of the kingdom in writing. The Kauravas were not miffed with the demand; they were upset enough to go to war because of the way the share had been demanded.

I made a number of enemies at D:FY by the manner of content delivery instead of the content delivery itself.

At D:FY, 'Temper' became my middle name. It wasn't just the impatience with which one responded, it was the tone that often dented the chassis. I recall a conversation towards the end that led to Rajiv saying, 'I quit'. I launched deep into him.

Looking back, I never put myself in anyone's shoes. I spoke from the perspective of my shoes, period. And much of my venom was being derived from the frustration of how the pitch was crumbling even before we could bat.

I apologized later, but the water had flowed under the bridge by then.

Greenlight

Marne se pehle jeena mat chhodo

Life can be decoded from an understanding of the past, but must always be lived in the present. Besides, only time can heal what reason cannot. The sad part was that for long I chose not to reason. As a child, I accepted loss faster than most; never sulked when I lost because, looking back, this could well have arisen from low self-esteem where one had reconciled to the fact that one could never win.

This perspective resurfaced when D:FY floundered. This time the loss was massive; this time the toll was financial and emotional; this time it was like losing a family member after prolonged illness.

Interestingly, despite losing Rs 30 crore in thirty months, I moved on easily for an interesting reason: the urgency to enhance life stability, which represented a new challenge. This need for some calm in life proved to be my next 'project', and hence, I moved on.

I reached out to Atul Kapur and Sameer Sain, co-founders of Everstone (Singapore-headquartered private investment firm with whom I had worked between 2006 and 2008). Since I had never put my CV out on the market through HR consultants, the idea was to reach out to those familiar with my capability. Sameer and Atul ticked the boxes; they were based in Singapore. I messaged Atul with a brief narrative of my D:FY failure and asked if I could work at Everstone Group. He called that evening and reconnected with warmth. He asked me what I wanted to do. I told him about my experience as an entrepreneur and in the Indian public markets. Atul said, 'Let's connect next week when I am in India.'

When I walked into Everstone's office a week later, Sameer was present. Sameer asked me the same question: 'What do you want to do next?' The upshot was that Sameer asked me to spend time with him in Singapore. Round two of the discussion transpired in Singapore the following week. Sameer viewed me as almost the same Prashant who had left him in 2008; he recalled the Prashant that had been, my need to create quick wealth and trading equities that distracted me from work; I countered by saying that the D:FY debacle had been a transformation.

Sameer picked on that word 'transformation'. He narrated how Everstone had diversified beyond private equity to industrial real estate (largest in India by far), green infrastructure (joint venture with British Petroleum and the Indian government), venture capital and credit. He spoke about a lot that needed to be done. He spoke about my role as a 'breadth' player. He spoke about how I could work closely with him on building Brand Everstone. He spoke about how my capital market experience could be leveraged for some Everstone-promoted companies going public. He finally said something that made an impression: 'PD, this is your home. I have always liked you – not your hurry-to-create-wealth attitude. Trust me and hop on. *Bahut kuch karenge saath mein'* (There is a lot we will do together).

This is your home. That line did it. I joined Everstone in September 2019.

One of my first assignments was an evaluation of one of their prominent investee companies called Burger King India, which was planning an IPO. After spending time on the company and engaging with the CEO, Raj Varman, I called Sameer. I told him that I needed to move on to Burger King. The story was brilliant, the CEO and team were great, but no one within possessed any public markets experience. Within a couple of months, I was seconded to Burger King India to drive its engagement with potential investors.

Some of the old excitement was now returning; I was confident of positioning Burger King India differently from other listed burger chains. The more time I spent talking to the Burger King India team, the more my confidence returned. We had a compelling growth story to be showcased to investors. After a number of years, I reconnected with the investor fraternity. I was back in the game.

We scheduled an extensive global and Indian road show (the term for investment bankers taking a company on a city-hopping tour to meet prospective investors). CEO Raj Varman, CFO Sumit Zaveri and I travelled across cities in India, Singapore, Hong Kong, London and the US from January 2020 onwards. In a month, we attended more than 200 investor meetings. And just when we were about to launch, the COVID-19 pandemic was unleashed. Three days to the IPO, the Indian government announced a lockdown, the stock market collapsed and we were compelled to call off the offering.

They say distance lends observation to the view and so it happened in my case. During lockdown I began to think of how my life would have evolved had I not closed D:FY.

If we had opted for financial investors: My personal mortgage would have been rescued. We would have corrected our business mistakes. We would have ordered for Season Three. We would have widened our distribution network (offline and online). We would have expanded the team. And then we would have run into COVID-19. That lockdown, starting March 2020, would have broken our back, our investors would have lost money and faith and we would have been compelled to bleed and call the show off well into the lockdown.

If we had merged into Future Group's brand: Future Group could not survive high debt and the personal debt of the promoter Biyani's family. The value of their holding declined by more than 80 per cent during the lockdown. Future Group sold out to Reliance Retail. As an extension, this is what would have happened to us: All D:FY shareholders would have got shares in Future Enterprises Limited, the surviving entity of FG (following our business being acquired by Reliance Retail). We would have received 20 per cent of the agreed value due to a decline in FG share prices. We would have salvaged a bit, but in the end it would still be curtains. It took the distant outbreak of a pandemic to convince me that shutting D:FY was the right decision (Jain, 2020).

Meanwhile, things were looking up at Burger King India. Recoveries were improving. The team used the delayed IPO as an opportunity to transform the customer mindset and experience. The equity markets began to revive. When we spoke to our investment bankers on reviving the IPO process, they appeared sceptical.

Then came that evening call.

In late September 2020, Sameer Sain took a massive call that reminded me of a quote from Shakespeare, 'There is a tide in the affairs of men which, taken at the flood, leads on to fortune; Omitted, all the voyage of their life is bound in shallows and in miseries.'

He said: 'Let's go for it.' There was a spring in his voice. We decided to re-initiate the IPO.

By October 2020, restaurants were getting operational; footfalls were reviving.

Raj would share our story – morning calls with prospective Hong Kong and Singapore investors, India meetings after noon, then London in the evening, and with barely a two-hour break, we would be ready for the US. We presented to over 300+ institutional investors. We e-met family offices. We e-met large high net worth individuals (HNIs). We e-met portfolio fund managers.

The marquee institutional investor demand (qualitative and quantitative, global and Indian) for Burger King India stock began to build. The press conference was well attended. The broker meet was a success (750 attended). We launched the IPO on 2 December 2020. The question was not whether the IPO would be subscribed; the question was 'By how many times?'

Greenlight

Then came 4 December 2020, the last day of the IPO. I nervously entered the Burger King India office (Marol, Andheri East, Mumbai). Expectations were high. Calls kept coming from colleagues, family and friends. We communicated the IPO subscription status 'live' at the office. Even though we had mobilized what we had wanted in just two hours, we were playing a different game now – the game of 'number of times of oversubscription' that would validate the strength of our brand and our ability to communicate.

In another country, India had been asked to bat by Australia in the first T-20 and struggled for fourteen of twenty overs. The TV screen showed a worried Virat Kohli; deep inside I was nervous as well. The slog overs were starting for India; the slog overs were starting for Burger King India as well.

The equity markets shut at 3.30 p.m.; the BSE Sensex touched an all-time high of 45,000. The next ninety minutes were critical for us. Australia was 55-0 in seven overs. India went on to win. Burger King India's IPO was oversubscribed 157 times. We had sought Rs 810 crore, we received investor offering of more than Rs 70,000 crore.

The show – my show – had received a decisive extension; I had lived to fight another day.

More importantly, the share price of my life – bullish at first, bearish thereafter – had found dependable support to revert to its growth journey.

The best, I keep telling myself, is yet to be.

*Greenlights** by Matthew McConaughey sums it up all so beautifully for me.

Greenlights mean go – advance, carry on, continue. They say proceed. Greenlights can also be disguised as yellow and red lights.

Navigating the autobahn of life in the best way possible is about getting relative with the inevitable at the right time.

The inevitability of a situation is not relative; when we accept the outcome of a given situation as inevitable, then how we chose to deal with it is relative. We either persist and continue in our present pursuit of a desired result, pivot and take a new track to get it, or concede altogether and tally one up for fate. We push on, call the audible, or wave the white flag and live to fight another day. The secret to our satisfaction lies in which one of these we choose to do when. This is the art of livin.

---

* McConaughey, Matthew (2020), *Greenlights: Raucous Stories and Outlaw Wisdom from the Academy Award-winning Actor*, New York: Crown

Sources

ANTA (April 2021). *Investor Relations.* Retrieved from anta.com: https://ir.anta.com/en/financial.php?open=h#f3

Money Control (2014). 'FTIL jumps 6%; Prashant Desai replaces Jignesh as CEO, MD.' Retrieved from moneycontrol.com: https://www.moneycontrol.com/news/business/stocks/ftil-jumps-6-prashant-desai-replaces-jignesh-as-ceo-md-1551879.html

Trisys (2021, April). Retrieved from trisyscom.com: https://www.trisyscom.com/

Canton Fair (2021). Retrieved from cantonfair: https://www.cantonfair.org.cn/en/

Forbes (4 April 2021). *Profile.* Retrieved from forbes.com: https://www.forbes.com/profile/rakesh-jhunjhunwala/?sh=4ec91bdd174b

Fryer, B. (2003). 'Storytelling that moves people.' *Harvard Business Review*.

Jain, S. (2020). 'Mukesh Ambani buys Big Bazaar: Future Group's retail, wholesale, logistic biz sold to Reliance Retail.' *Financial Express*.

Balaram Chini Mills Limited (April 2021). *Investor Corner*. Retrieved from http://chini.com/investor_finnancial/: http://chini.com

MCX (2012). *About Us – Award and Recognition*. Retrieved from mcxindia: https://www.mcxindia.com/about-us/awards-recognition

Nikhil Jain, L.P. (2021). *LinkedIn*. Retrieved from LinkedIn: https://www.linkedin.com/in/nikhil-jain-8711a17/

Pensole (2021). *Our Story*. Retrieved from Pensole: https://pensole.com/explore/our-story/

Punj, S. (2021). 'I was the first one to make push button phones in India: Sunil Bharti Mittal.' *India Today*.

Schultz, K. (2011). *Being Wrong: Adventures in the Margin of Error*. HarperCollins Publishers.

Sinha, P. (2013). 'NSEL halts trading, spooks investors.' *Times of India*.

Scroll (27 September 2018). Amazon's Indian web series 'Inside Edge' nominated for International Emmy Award. Retrieved from Scroll: https://scroll.in/reel/896124/amazons-indian-web-series-inside-edge-nominated-for-international-emmy-award

Sixth Sense Ventures (April 2021). *Team*. Retrieved from Sixth Sense Ventures: http://sixthsenseventures.com/team/nikhil-vora/

Index

231

About the Author

Prashant Desai is a senior director at Everstone Group, a leading India-focused South East Asia private firm with investments across private equity, real estate, green energy and venture capital. He is currently the head of strategy and investor relations at Burger King India.

Prashant is also a trained speed reader and a half marathoner with forty timed runs. He is dedicated to spreading financial literacy through his social media channels. You may reach out to Prashant on Instagram @itsprashantdesai.